Bridge to Terabithia
Novel Literature Unit Study and Lapbook

**Unit Study Created
by Teresa Ives Lilly**

www.hshighlights.com

This unit can be used in any grade level in which students are able to read the book. The activities are best used in grades 2 to 6. Almost everything in the unit can be used to create a file folder lap book. Each unit study covers one whole book and includes:

Comprehension Activities:
Fill in the Blanks, True and False, Multiple Choice, Who, What, Where, When, Why and How Questions.

Pre-Reading Skills Activities
Author Information Activity, Time line Activity, Theater Box Activity

Lesson Activities
Encyclopedia, Journal, Vocabulary, Sequence of Events, Handwriting
Main Idea, Key Event, Prediction, Comparison,

Literature Skills Activity
Main Character, Main Setting, Main Problem, Possible Solutions, Character Traits, Character Interaction, Cause and Effect, Description, Pyramid of Importance, Villain vs. Hero

Poetry Skills Activity
Couplet, Triplet, Quinzain, Haiku, Cinquain, Tanka, Diamanté, Lantern and Shape Poem

Newspaper Writing Activity
Editorial, Travel, Advice Column, Comics, Society News, Sports, Obituary, Weddings, Book Review, Wanted Ads, Word Search

Creative Writing Activity
Letter, Fairy Tale, Mystery, Science Fiction, Fable, Dream or Nightmare, Tall Tale, Memoir, Newberry Award, A Different Ending.

Writing Skills Activity
Description, Expository, Dialogue, Process, Point of View, Persuasion, Compare and Contrast, Sequel, Climax and Plot Analysis.

Poster Board Activity
Collage, Theater Poster, Wanted Poster, Coat of Arms, Story Quilt, Chalk Art, Silhouette, Board Game Construction, Door Sign, Jeopardy.

Art Expression Activity
Main Character, Main Setting, Travel Brochure, Postal Stamp, Book Cover, Menu, Fashion Designer, Puzzle, Mini Book, Ten Commandments.

Creative Art Activity
Sculpture, Shadow Box, Mosaic, Mobile, Acrostic, Tapestry, Paper Dolls, Book Mark, Photography, Parade Float, Sketch

Other Activities:
Sign Language Vocabulary, Literature Web, Bingo.

Published at www.hshighlights.com
Copyright © 2009 All rights reserved
Teachers may make copies for their individual students only

How to do the Lapbook Activity: To use this unit study either print out all the pages or Student wills recreate most of them in a notebook or on white or colored paper.

All of the pages can be added to the lapbook project as shown in the photos, or only use those items you want to have students create a lapbook and have them use a spiral notebook for the other pages.

The following are photos of how the work can be presented in the lapbook format. To create the lapbook use 3-6 file folders (colored are best), construction paper or index cards, markers, glue and a stapler.

Front

Back

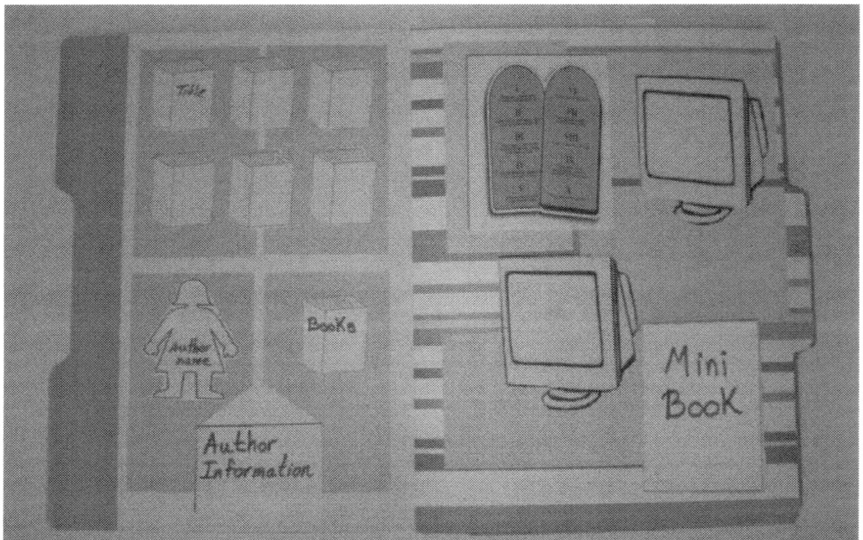
Title
Author name
Books
Author Information
Mini Book

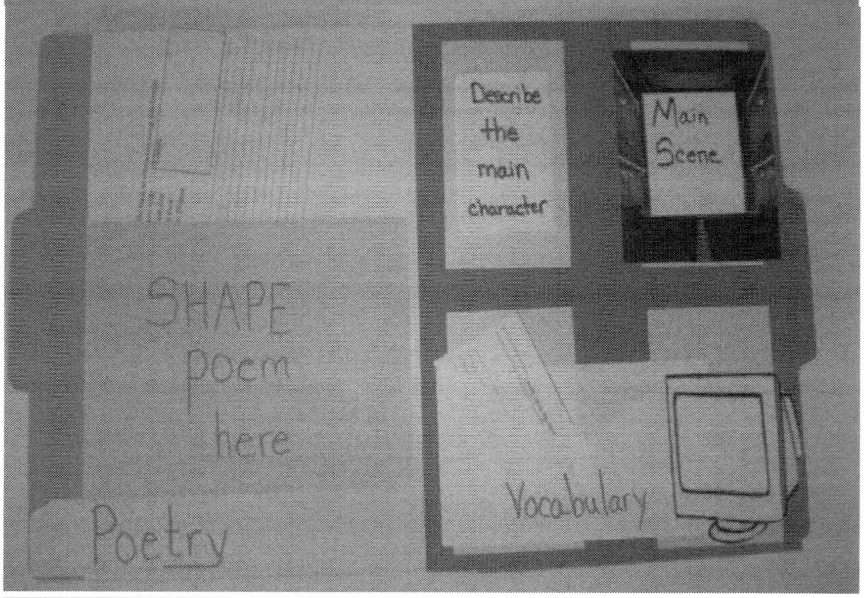
Describe the main character
Main Scene
SHAPE poem here
Vocabulary
Poetry

Postal Stamp
Writing Skills
Sequence

Encyclopedia
Fashion
Design
Illustrate New Book Cover
Journal

Creative writing
Literature Activities

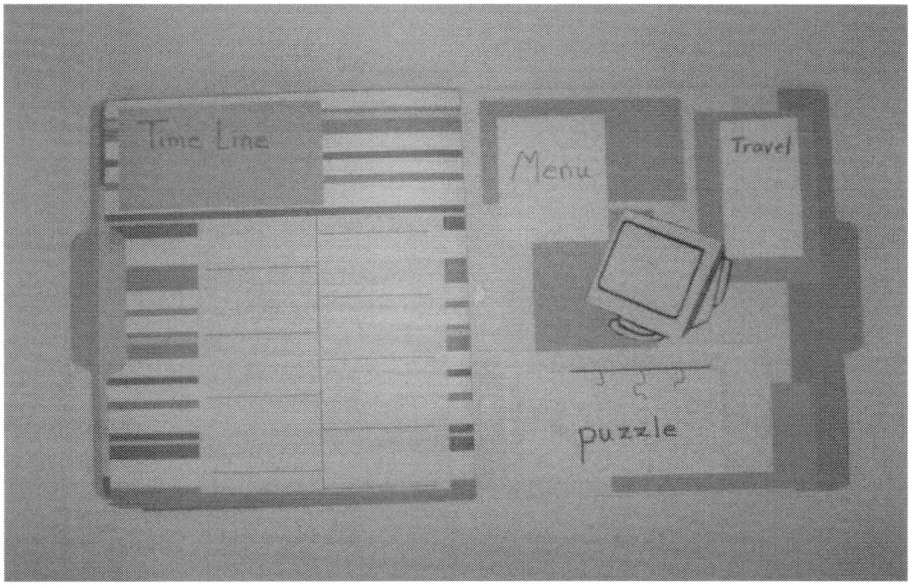
Time Line
Menu
Travel
puzzle

How to do the Newspaper Activity: As the student completes the news paper activities, have student lay the completed work out on a big board or on several poster boards. Don't have them glue the items on the board until the entire newspaper is completed and all sections are put where the student wants them to be. Have student create a name for their newspaper. Then have them type out the name, in big bold letters and place it on the top of the board. with tape or sticky clay. Then tape of stick all the completed articles onto board as well.

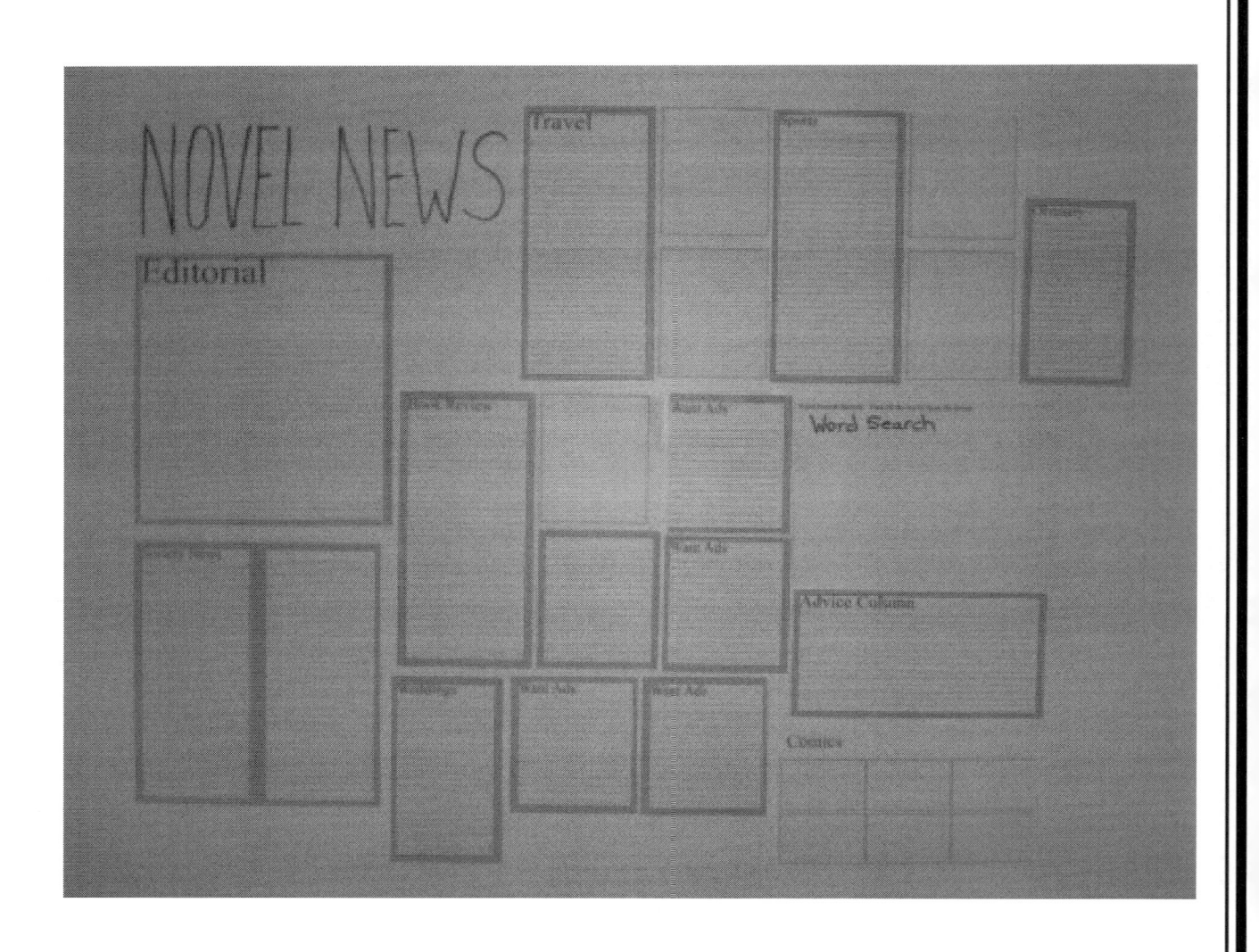

Pre-Reading Activities

Pre-Reading Activity: Student will look at the book they will be studying for this unit. Then student will write the information required for this activity on the following book patterns or in their notebook. The patterns may be cut out and placed on the lapbook.

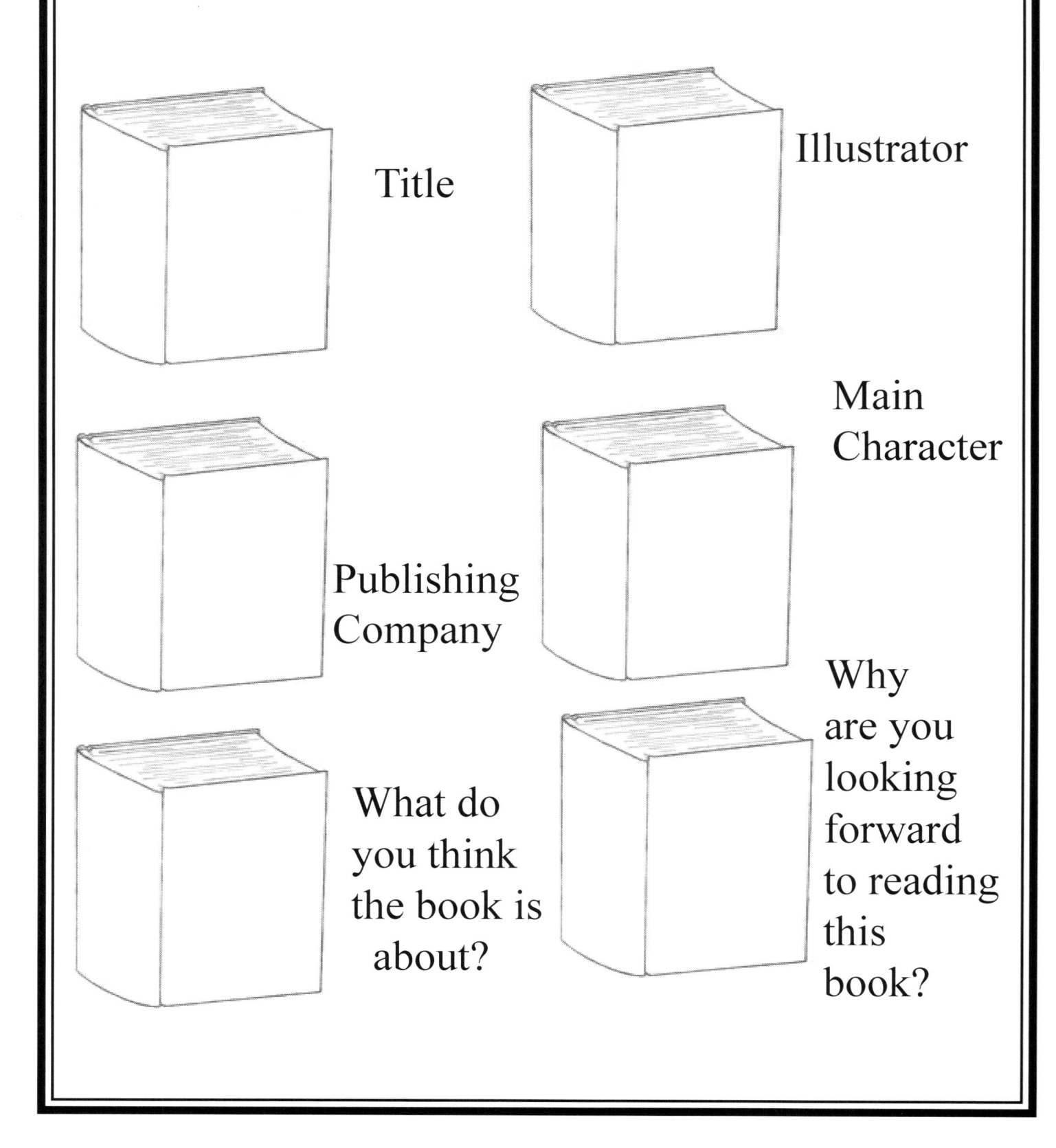

Title

Illustrator

Publishing Company

Main Character

What do you think the book is about?

Why are you looking forward to reading this book?

Author Activity: Student will use the book they are studying and information found on the internet to find out information about the author. Then student will write the information required for this activity on the patterns or in their notebook. The patterns may be cut out and placed on the lapbook.

Student will write the author's name on the correct pattern and the author's age.

Student will rite the name of all the books written by this author on the book pattern. If there are more than three books, just select the three most famous.

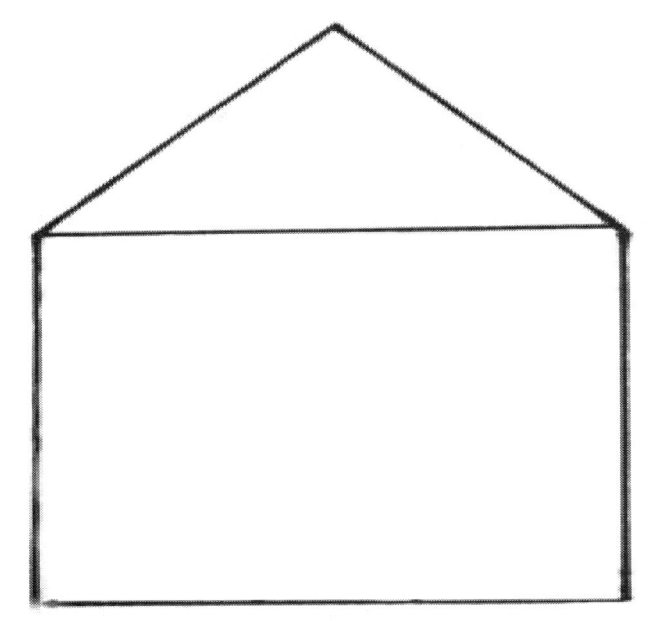

Student will write information about the author on the house pattern, such as where the author was born, lived and how they became an author.

Time Line Activity: Student will use the book they are studying to fill out the time line indicating when anything new, interesting or important happens in the book. This time line pattern can be copied into the student's notebook or this pattern can be printed smaller and placed on the lapbook.

All Vocabulary Lists, Comprehension Questions, True and False, Fill in the Blank for each lesson are at at the end of this unit study.

Lesson 1
Activities

Lesson 1 Activities: Students will use the book they are studying and information found on the internet for the following activities. Then the student will write the information required for this activity on the patterns or in their notebook. The patterns may be cut out and placed on the lapbook.

Encyclopedia:
Student will choose one subject from this lesson that interested them and look it up on the internet or in encyclopedia. They will write the name of the subject across the top of the monitor pattern. On the monitor screen section, they will write three or more interesting facts about the subject.

Journal:
Student will imagine that they are one of the characters from the story. After reading each lesson, they will write a short journal entry telling what happened from that character's point of view.
Student will also draw a picture to go along with the journal entry.
At the end of the book, student will staple all the journal entries together to form a complete booklet.
They can even create a special cover for it from construction paper.

Vocabulary word: _____
Definition of the word: _____
_____
_____

Antonym of the word: _____
How many syllables does the word have? _____

Vocabulary Word: _____
Sentence using the word: _____
_____
_____

Synonym of the word: _____

Vocabulary: Student will use the vocabulary words from the list for this lesson. On one of the patterns, or on one index card they will write one vocabulary word. They should also write the definition of the word, then the Antonym and how many Syllables the word has.

On the other card, the student will write the same word. They will write a full sentence using this word and then write the Synonym of the word.

They will repeat this for all the vocabulary words in this lesson.

Place the patterns or cards in an envelope which can be glued into the student's notebook or onto the lapbook..

Sequencing: At the end of the lesson the student will write two of the main events on these two strips. Save them in an envelope which can be glued onto the lapbook or in the notebook. At the end of the book, these strips can be taken out and the student can arrange them in the correct order as they occurred in the story.

Handwriting: Student will pick their favorite sentence that they read in this lesson. Have them write the sentence in their best handwriting on this page or in their notebook.

Student will write out the answers for the following:

Main Idea: In a sentence or two, write what the main idea was of this section.
_____
_____
_____
_____
_____
_____

Key Event: In a sentence or two write what the most important event was in this section.
_____
_____
_____
_____
_____
_____

Prediction: In a sentence of two write what you Predict will happen in the next section.
_____
_____
_____
_____
_____
_____

Comparison: In a sentence of two compare two things in this section. Tell what makes them alike and what makes them different.
_____
_____
_____
_____
_____
_____

Fact or Opinion: In one sentence write a fact about this section and one sentence that is an opinion about the lesson.
_____
_____
_____
_____
_____
_____

Literature Skills: Main Character: Student will write words in the circles to describe the main character.

Physical appearance

Concern or worry

Main character

Who they relate to

Your opinion of them

Poetry Form: Student will write a poem about the book or characters using this format.

Couplet: A Couplet is a two line poem with a fun and simple rhyming pattern. Each line has the same number of syllables and their endings must rhyme with one another. Humor is often used in couplets.

Example:
   If a seed could have its way
   it would grow in just one day.

Newspaper Activity: Student will use this form to write their newspaper piece on then paste it onto their newspaper lay out poster.

Editorial: An editorial is written by the editor of the newspaper. In an editorial the editor gives an opinion of something. Student will imagine that they are the editor of their newspaper. Student will write their opinion of something that happened in the book so far.

Editorial

Creative Writing Activity: Student will use this form or write in their notebook.

Letter Writing: Student will write a letter from one character in the book to another character in the book.

Dear   ,

Sincerely,

Writing Skills Activity: Student will use this form or write in their notebook.

Descriptive: Descriptive writing uses words such as color and texture to describe something. Student will describe a person, place or thing from the lesson.

Lapbook Activity: **Main Character:** Student will draw and color a picture of the main character on the solid section of the flap book. Student will cut out the entire flap book on the dotted lines and fold the four flap sections over the picture of the main character. On the outside of each flap student will write different words that describes the character; one word per flap.

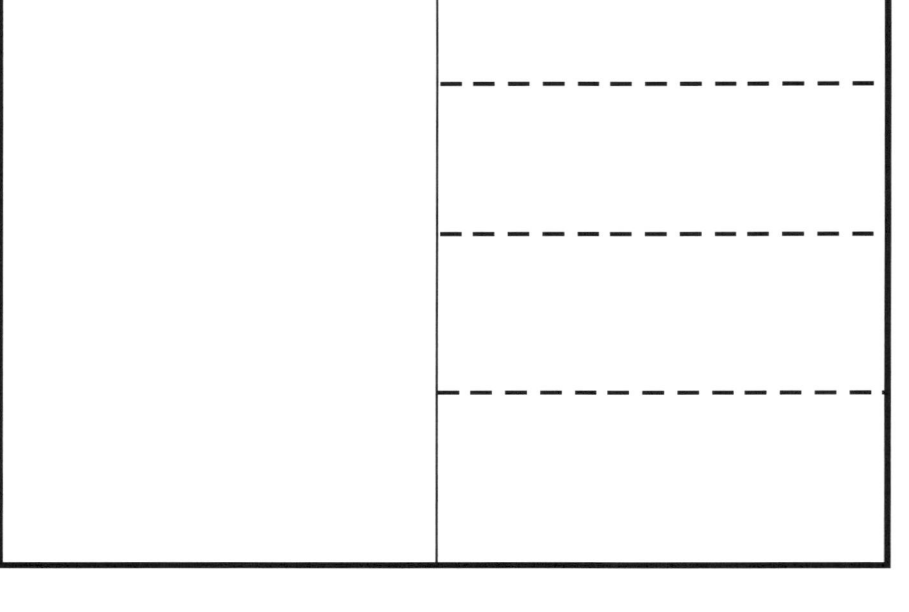

Poster Board Activity:
Book Collage
Student will print out pictures from the internet that represent characters from the story. They can use magazine pictures as well. Then student will glue these pictures all over a 1/2 poster board in an over lapping fashion to create a book collage.

Creative Art Activity:
Sculpting
Student will create on of the characters from the story out of clay or play doe.

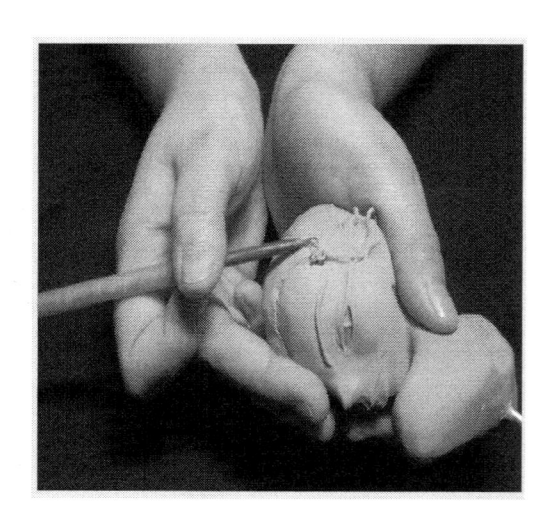

Lesson 2
Activities

Lesson 2 Activities: Students will use the book they are studying and information found on the internet for the following activities. Then the student will write the information required for this activity on the patterns or in their notebook. The patterns may be cut out and placed on the lapbook.

Encyclopedia:
Student will choose one subject from this lesson that interested them and look it up on the internet or in encyclopedia. They will write the name of the subject across the top of the monitor pattern. On the monitor screen section, they will write three or more interesting facts about the subject.

Journal:
Student will imagine that they are one of the characters from the story. After reading each lesson, they will write a short journal entry telling what happened from that character's point of view.
Student will also draw a picture to go along with the journal entry.
At the end of the book, student will staple all the journal entries together to form a complete booklet.
They can even create a special cover for it from construction paper.

Vocabulary word: _____
Definition of the word: _____
_____
_____

Antonym of the word: _____
How many syllables does the word have? _____

Vocabulary Word: _____
Sentence using the word: _____
_____
_____

Synonym of the word: _____

Vocabulary: Student will use the vocabulary words from the list for this lesson. On one of the patterns, or on one index card they will write one vocabulary word. They should also write the definition of the word, then the Antonym and how many Syllables the word has.

On the other card, the student will write the same word. They will write a full sentence using this word and then write the Synonym of the word.

They will repeat this for all the vocabulary words in this lesson.

Place the patterns or cards in an envelope which can be glued into the student's notebook or onto the lapbook..

Sequencing: At the end of the lesson the student will write two of the main events on these two strips. Save them in an envelope which can be glued onto the lapbook or in the notebook. At the end of the book, these strips can be taken out and the student can arrange them in the correct order as they occurred in the story.

Handwriting: Student will pick their favorite sentence that they read in this lesson. Have them write the sentence in their best handwriting on this page or in their notebook.

Student will write out the answers for the following:

Main Idea: In a sentence or two, write what the main idea was of this section.

Key Event: In a sentence or two write what the most important event was in this section.

Prediction: In a sentence of two write what you Predict will happen in the next section.

Comparison: In a sentence of two compare two things in this section. Tell what makes them alike and what makes them different.

Fact or Opinion: In one sentence write a fact about this section and one sentence that is an opinion about the lesson.

Main Setting: Student will fill in the information to describe the main setting and to describe the minor settings in the story.

What is the main setting? _____

Describe it _____

Describe a Minor Setting

_____

Describe a Minor Setting

_____

Poetry Form: Student will write a poem about the book or characters using this format.

Triplet:
Triplets are three-lined poems that rhyme. Each line has the same number of Syllables.

Example:
 The bunny hops and hops
 Til all at once she stops
 To munch some carrot tops.

Newspaper Activity: Student will use this form to write their newspaper piece on then paste it onto their newspaper lay out poster.

Travel Section: Student should imagine they write the travel column for a newspaper. Student should write a short article about traveling to the area where this book takes place. Student should find one or two photos on the internet that reminds them of this place and place it on the newspaper lay out poster as well.

Travel

Creative Writing Activity: Student will use this form or write in their notebook.

Fairy Tales : Fairy Tales are fanciful tales of legendary deeds and creatures, usually intended for children. Student will write a fairy tale involving one of the characters from the story and illustrate it.

Writing Skills Activity: Student will use this form or write in their notebook.

Persuasion: Persuasion is a way of writing, in which you convince someone of something. Student will write to try to persuade someone in the story to do something differently than they did in the story.

Lapbook Activity: Main Setting : Student will draw and color the main scene or main setting of this story for a play in this stage scene. Place in lapbook.

Poster Board Activity:
Theater Poster
Student will create a poster that may be found outside of a theater which is putting on a play of this book.

Creative Art Activity:
Shadow Box:
Student will use a shoe box turned on its side to create a scene from the book in using pictures from the internet or other small items.

Lesson 3
Activities

Lesson 3 Activities: Students will use the book they are studying and information found on the internet for the following activities. Then the student will write the information required for this activity on the patterns or in their notebook. The patterns may be cut out and placed on the lapbook.

Encyclopedia:
Student will choose one subject from this lesson that interested them and look it up on the internet or in encyclopedia. They will write the name of the subject across the top of the monitor pattern. On the monitor screen section, they will write three or more interesting facts about the subject.

Journal:
Student will imagine that they are one of the characters from the story. After reading each lesson, they will write a short journal entry telling what happened from that character's point of view.
Student will also draw a picture to go along with the journal entry.
At the end of the book, student will staple all the journal entries together to form a complete booklet.
They can even create a special cover for it from construction paper.

Vocabulary word: _____
Definition of the word: _____
_____
_____

Antonym of the word: _____
How many syllables does the word have? _____

Vocabulary Word: _____
Sentence using the word: _____
_____
_____

Synonym of the word: _____

Vocabulary: Student will use the vocabulary words from the list for this lesson. On one of the patterns, or on one index card they will write one vocabulary word. They should also write the definition of the word, then the Antonym and how many Syllables the word has.

On the other card, the student will write the same word. They will write a full sentence using this word and then write the Synonym of the word.

They will repeat this for all the vocabulary words in this lesson.

Place the patterns or cards in an envelope which can be glued into the student's notebook or onto the lapbook..

Sequencing: At the end of the lesson the student will write two of the main events on these two strips. Save them in an envelope which can be glued onto the lapbook or in the notebook. At the end of the book, these strips can be taken out and the student can arrange them in the correct order as they occurred in the story.

Handwriting: Student will pick their favorite sentence that they read in this lesson. Have them write the sentence in their best handwriting on this page or in their notebook.

Student will write out the answers for the following:
Main Idea: In a sentence or two, write what the main idea was of this section.

Key Event: In a sentence or two write what the most important event was in this section.

Prediction: In a sentence of two write what you Predict will happen in the next section.

Comparison: In a sentence of two compare two things in this section. Tell what makes them alike and what makes them different.

Fact or Opinion: In one sentence write a fact about this section and one sentence that is an opinion about the lesson.

Main Problem: Most stories seem to have one main problem. There may be other small problems, but there is an overall large problem. Student will write what the main problem is in the larger rectangle, and some of the smaller problems in the smaller ones.

Poetry Form: Student will write a poem about the book or characters using this format.

Quinzain: Quinzains are unrhymed three line poems that contain 15 syllables. The pattern is: The first line is 7, the second is 5 and the third is 3. The first line makes a statement and the next two lines ask a question about the subject.

Example:
   I like to write poetry
   would you like to write
   a poem too?

Newspaper Activity: Student will use this form to write their newspaper piece on then paste it onto their newspaper lay out poster.

Wanted Ads Section: Student will create several wanted ads that characters in the story might post in a newspaper or ads the characters might answer.

Wanted Ad

Wanted Ad

Wanted Ad

Wanted Ad

Creative Writing Activity: Student will use this form or write in their notebook.

Mystery: Student will write a mystery that may occur in this story or to the characters in this story and then illustrate it.

Writing Skills Activity: Student will use this form or write in their notebook.

Expository: Expository writing is writing strictly to inform. Student will write an expository piece that informs someone about an event that happened in the story.

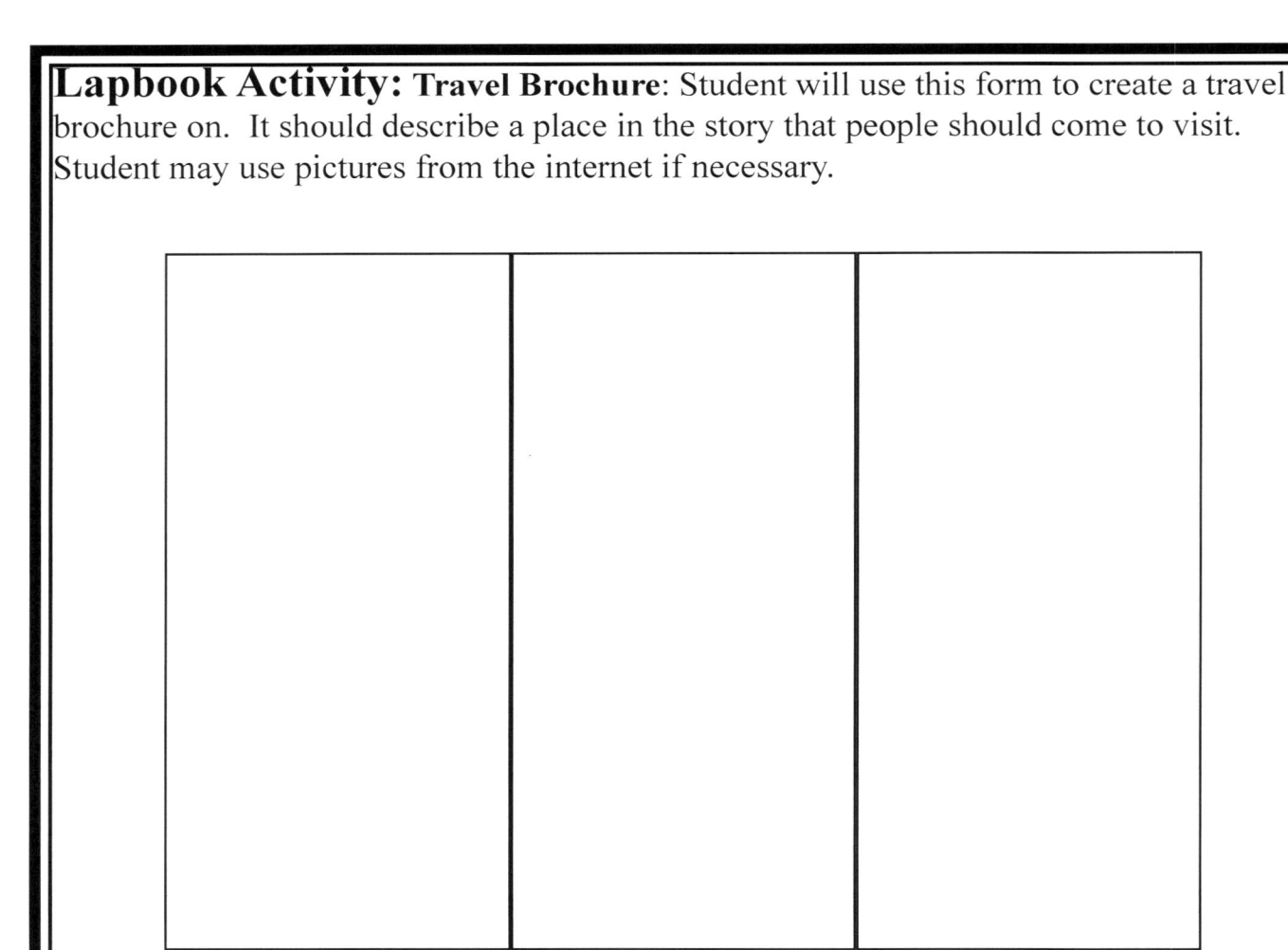

Lapbook Activity: Travel Brochure: Student will use this form to create a travel brochure on. It should describe a place in the story that people should come to visit. Student may use pictures from the internet if necessary.

Poster Board Activity:
Wanted Poster
Student will create a "Wanted by the Law," poster for one of the villains in the story.

Creative Art Activity:
Mosaic Plate
Student will create a mosaic scene from the story on a paper plate using small pieces of construction paper glued in a mosaic fashion.

Lesson 4
Activities

Lesson 4 Activities: Students will use the book they are studying and information found on the internet for the following activities. Then the student will write the information required for this activity on the patterns or in their notebook. The patterns may be cut out and placed on the lapbook.

Encyclopedia:
Student will choose one subject from this lesson that interested them and look it up on the internet or in encyclopedia. They will write the name of the subject across the top of the monitor pattern. On the monitor screen section, they will write three or more interesting facts about the subject.

Journal:
Student will imagine that they are one of the characters from the story. After reading each lesson, they will write a short journal entry telling what happened from that character's point of view.
Student will also draw a picture to go along with the journal entry.
At the end of the book, student will staple all the journal entries together to form a complete booklet.
They can even create a special cover for it from construction paper.

Vocabulary word: _____
Definition of the word: _____
_____
_____

Antonym of the word: _____
How many syllables does the word have? _____

Vocabulary Word: _____
Sentence using the word: _____
_____
_____

Synonym of the word: _____

Vocabulary: Student will use the vocabulary words from the list for this lesson. On one of the patterns, or on one index card they will write one vocabulary word. They should also write the definition of the word, then the Antonym and how many Syllables the word has.

On the other card, the student will write the same word. They will write a full sentence using this word and then write the Synonym of the word.

They will repeat this for all the vocabulary words in this lesson.

Place the patterns or cards in an envelope which can be glued into the student's notebook or onto the lapbook..

Sequencing: At the end of the lesson the student will write two of the main events on these two strips. Save them in an envelope which can be glued onto the lapbook or in the notebook. At the end of the book, these strips can be taken out and the student can arrange them in the correct order as they occurred in the story.

Handwriting: Student will pick their favorite sentence that they read in this lesson. Have them write the sentence in their best handwriting on this page or in their notebook.

Student will write out the answers for the following:
Main Idea: In a sentence or two, write what the main idea was of this section.
_____
_____
_____
_____
_____
_____

Key Event: In a sentence or two write what the most important event was in this section.
_____
_____
_____
_____
_____
_____
_____

Prediction: In a sentence of two write what you Predict will happen in the next section.
_____
_____
_____
_____
_____
_____

Comparison: In a sentence of two compare two things in this section. Tell what makes them alike and what makes them different.
_____
_____
_____
_____
_____
_____

Fact or Opinion: In one sentence write a fact about this section and one sentence that is an opinion about the lesson.
_____
_____
_____
_____
_____
_____

Possible Solutions: Problems in a story can have several solutions. Student will write what some of the problems are in the story and possible solution in the shapes.

Problem:

Solution:

Problem:

Solution:

Problem:

Solution:

Poetry Form: Student will write a poem about the book or characters using this format.

Haiku: A haiku is a Japanese poem with no rhyme. Haiku poems have only three lines, each with a certain number of syllables.

Here is the pattern:
Line 1 = 5 syllables
Line 2 = 7 syllables
Line 3 = 5 syllables

Example:
Lion cubs doze in
shade, under shrubs, hidden from
hungry hyenas

Newspaper Activity: Student will use this form to write their newspaper piece on then paste it onto their newspaper lay out poster.

Advice Column Section: Student will come up with a question or concern that one of the characters in the story may have. The student will write a letter to the advice column and the advice column writer will answer.

Advice Column

Creative Writing Activity: Student will use this form or write in their notebook.

Science Fiction: Science Fiction stories take place in the far future usually in space or on earth in an advanced society. Student will write a science fiction story about the future of one of the characters and illustrate it.

Writing Skills Activity: Student will use this form or write in their notebook.

Dialogue: A dialogue is a conversation between two characters. Student will write a dialogue that could occur between two characters in the story. Student should use correct quotation marks.

Lapbook Activity: Postal Stamp: Student will create a new postal stamp for next year which would represent the book or characters of the book.

Poster Board Activity:
Coat of Arms
Using a poster board, student will create a coat of arms with a design to represent this story or a character in the story.

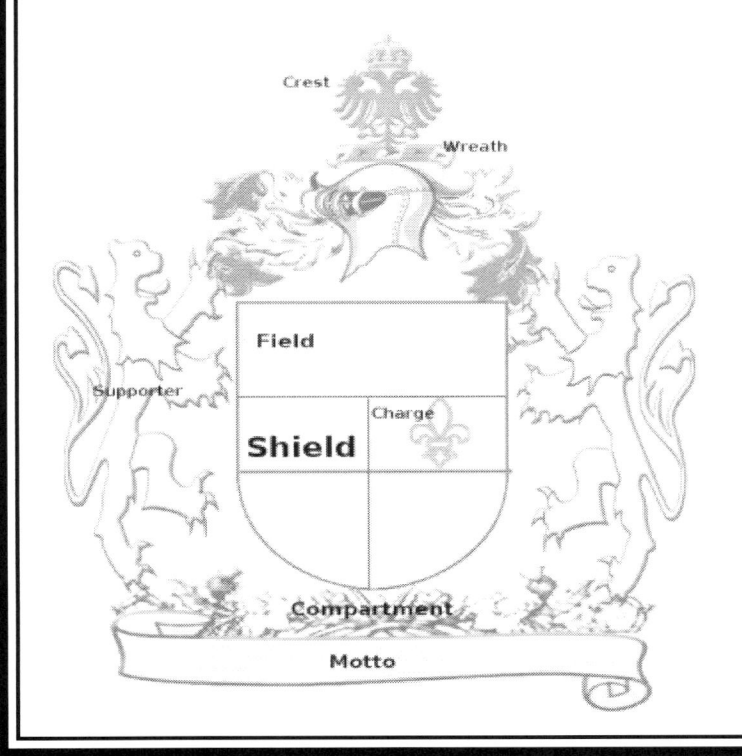

Creative Art Activity:
Mobile
Student will cut out pictures from the internet of characters of items that represent those in the book and then glue them onto long strips of card board. These can be hung with string to make a mobile.

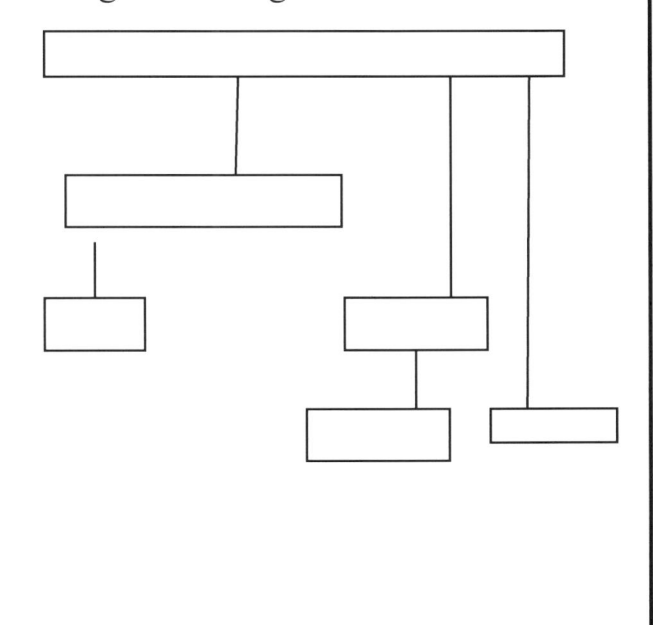

Lesson 5
Activities

Lesson 5 Activities: Students will use the book they are studying and information found on the internet for the following activities. Then the student will write the information required for this activity on the patterns or in their notebook. The patterns may be cut out and placed on the lapbook.

Encyclopedia:
Student will choose one subject from this lesson that interested them and look it up on the internet or in encyclopedia. They will write the name of the subject across the top of the monitor pattern. On the monitor screen section, they will write three or more interesting facts about the subject.

Journal:
Student will imagine that they are one of the characters from the story. After reading each lesson, they will write a short journal entry telling what happened from that character's point of view.
Student will also draw a picture to go along with the journal entry.
At the end of the book, student will staple all the journal entries together to form a complete booklet.
They can even create a special cover for it from construction paper.

Vocabulary word: _____
Definition of the word: _____
_____
_____

Antonym of the word: _____
How many syllables does the word have? _____

Vocabulary Word: _____
Sentence using the word: _____
_____
_____

Synonym of the word: _____

Vocabulary: Student will use the vocabulary words from the list for this lesson. On one of the patterns, or on one index card they will write one vocabulary word. They should also write the definition of the word, then the Antonym and how many Syllables the word has.

On the other card, the student will write the same word. They will write a full sentence using this word and then write the Synonym of the word.

They will repeat this for all the vocabulary words in this lesson.

Place the patterns or cards in an envelope which can be glued into the student's notebook or onto the lapbook..

Sequencing: At the end of the lesson the student will write two of the main events on these two strips. Save them in an envelope which can be glued onto the lapbook or in the notebook. At the end of the book, these strips can be taken out and the student can arrange them in the correct order as they occurred in the story.

Handwriting: Student will pick their favorite sentence that they read in this lesson. Have them write the sentence in their best handwriting on this page or in their notebook.

Student will write out the answers for the following:
Main Idea: In a sentence or two, write what the main idea was of this section.
_____
_____
_____
_____
_____
_____

Key Event: In a sentence or two write what the most important event was in this section.
_____
_____
_____
_____
_____
_____

Prediction: In a sentence of two write what you Predict will happen in the next section.
_____
_____
_____
_____
_____
_____

Comparison: In a sentence of two compare two things in this section. Tell what makes them alike and what makes them different.
_____
_____
_____
_____
_____

Fact or Opinion: In one sentence write a fact about this section and one sentence that is an opinion about the lesson.
_____
_____
_____
_____
_____
_____

Character Traits: In the circle for the Main Character Traits, student will write several of the main character's traits. In the circle for Student Traits, student will write several of the student's traits. Any traits that the main character and the student have in common should be in the area where the circles overlap called Common Traits.

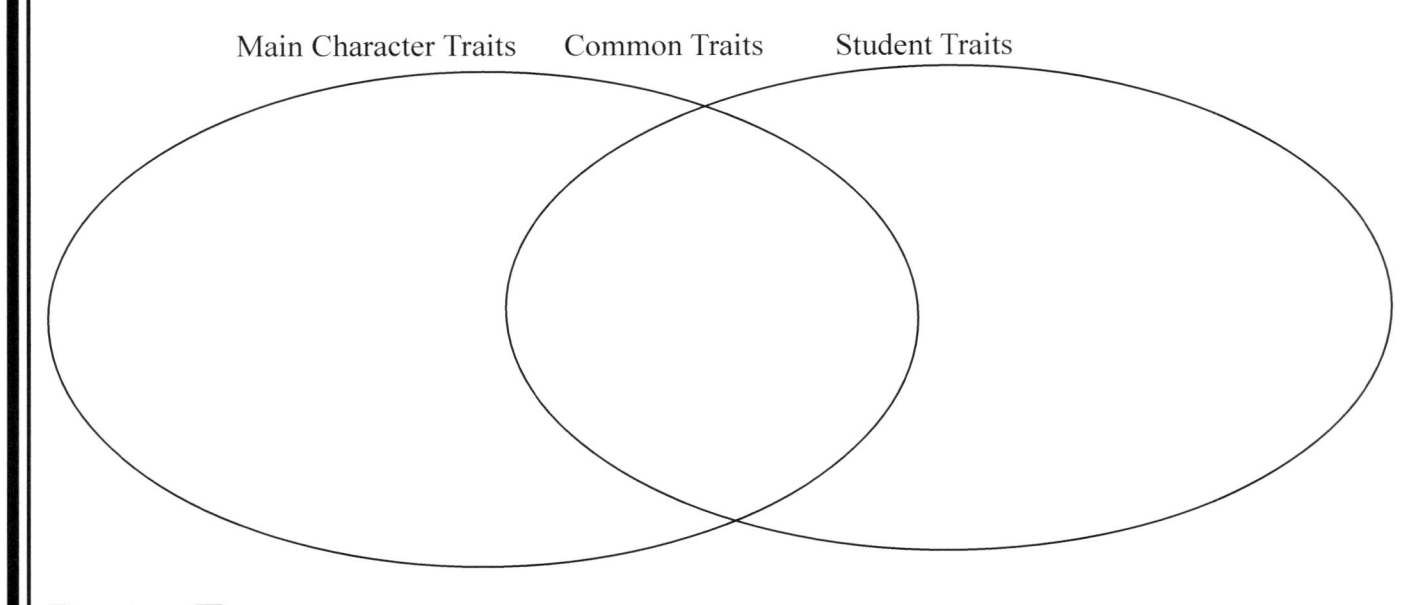

Main Character Traits   Common Traits   Student Traits

Poetry Form: Student will write a poem about the book or characters using this format.

Acrostic: In an acrostic poem the name of the person, object, or place is written vertically down the left hand side of the page. Each letter is capitalized and becomes the first letter of the word beginning each line. The words used should describe the person, object or place in a positive way. Each line may comprise a word, a phrase or a thought that is continued on to the next line.

Example:
CAT
Can you see their eyes
At night in the dark
They glow........

Newspaper Activity: Student will use this form to write their newspaper piece on then paste it onto their newspaper lay out poster.

Comic Section: Student will create a funny cartoon about one of the events of characters in the story. Illustrate and color it.

Comics

Creative Writing Activity: Student will use this form or write in their notebook.
Fable: A fable is a short, allegorical narrative, making a moral point, traditionally by means of animal characters that speak and act like humans. Student will write a fable that comes to mind while reading this story in which one of the characters from the book learns a moral from an animal. Then student will illustrate it.

Writing Skills Activity: Student will use this form or write in their notebook.

Process: Process writing is telling the actual steps it takes to do something. Student will write a step by step process that one of the characters in the book had to do to or should have done.

Lapbook Activity: Book Cover Illustrator:
Student will create their own book cover for this story on the form. Make sure to include the title, illustrator and publisher's name.

Poster Board Activity:
Story Quilt
Divide a poster board into eight to sixteen equal squares. In each square the student will draw different pictures to tell what has happened in the story so far.

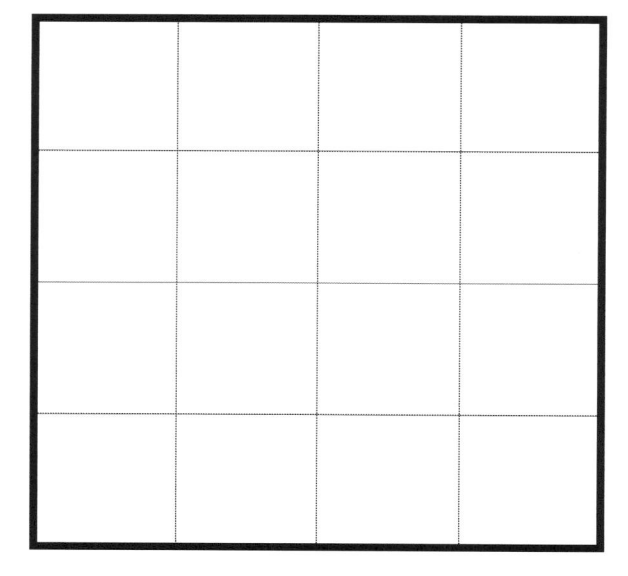

Creative Art Activity:
Tapestry
Using an 8 inch by 12 inch piece of felt as the background, student will cut out characters and items from the story from colored felt and glue onto the background to create a story tapestry.

Lapbook Activity: Book Cover Illustrator:

Lesson 6
Activities

Lesson 6 Activities: Students will use the book they are studying and information found on the internet for the following activities. Then the student will write the information required for this activity on the patterns or in their notebook. The patterns may be cut out and placed on the lapbook.

Encyclopedia:
Student will choose one subject from this lesson that interested them and look it up on the internet or in encyclopedia. They will write the name of the subject across the top of the monitor pattern. On the monitor screen section, they will write three or more interesting facts about the subject.

Journal:
Student will imagine that they are one of the characters from the story. After reading each lesson, they will write a short journal entry telling what happened from that character's point of view.
Student will also draw a picture to go along with the journal entry.
At the end of the book, student will staple all the journal entries together to form a complete booklet.
They can even create a special cover for it from construction paper.

Vocabulary word: _____
Definition of the word: _____
_____
_____

Antonym of the word: _____
How many syllables does the word have? _____

Vocabulary Word: _____
Sentence using the word: _____
_____
_____

Synonym of the word: _____

Vocabulary: Student will use the vocabulary words from the list for this lesson. On one of the patterns, or on one index card they will write one vocabulary word. They should also write the definition of the word, then the Antonym and how many Syllables the word has.

On the other card, the student will write the same word. They will write a full sentence using this word and then write the Synonym of the word.

They will repeat this for all the vocabulary words in this lesson.

Place the patterns or cards in an envelope which can be glued into the student's notebook or onto the lapbook..

Sequencing: At the end of the lesson the student will write two of the main events on these two strips. Save them in an envelope which can be glued onto the lapbook or in the notebook. At the end of the book, these strips can be taken out and the student can arrange them in the correct order as they occurred in the story.

Handwriting: Student will pick their favorite sentence they read in this lesson. Have them write the sentence in their best handwriting on this page or in their notebook.

Student will write out the answers for the following:
Main Idea: In a sentence or two, write what the main idea was of this section.

Key Event: In a sentence or two write what the most important event was in this section.

Prediction: In a sentence of two write what you Predict will happen in the next section.

Comparison: In a sentence of two compare two things in this section. Tell what makes them alike and what makes them different.

Fact or Opinion: In one sentence write a fact about this section and one sentence that is an opinion about the lesson.

Character Interaction: In the circles, student will write the names of the characters in the story and then draw arrows from each circle to other circles to represent which character interact with one another. Start with the Main Character in the center.

Poetry Form: Student will write a poem about the book or characters using this format.

Cinquain: A cinquain is a short, five-line, non rhyming poem which follows the following pattern:

First line - The title (one word)
2nd line - Describes the title (two words)
3rd line - Express action (three words)
4th line - A feeling or thought (four words)
5th line - A Synonym or close word for the title

Example:
Insect
six legs
usually have wings
a mostly helpful annoyance
Bee

Newspaper Activity: Student will use this form to write their newspaper piece on then paste it onto their newspaper lay out poster.

Obituary Section: Student will imagine that one or more of the characters in the book died and will write an obituary telling how they died.

Wedding Announcement Section: Student will imagine that one of the characters in the story will get married soon and will write the wedding announcement, telling who they will marry, where and when the wedding will take place.

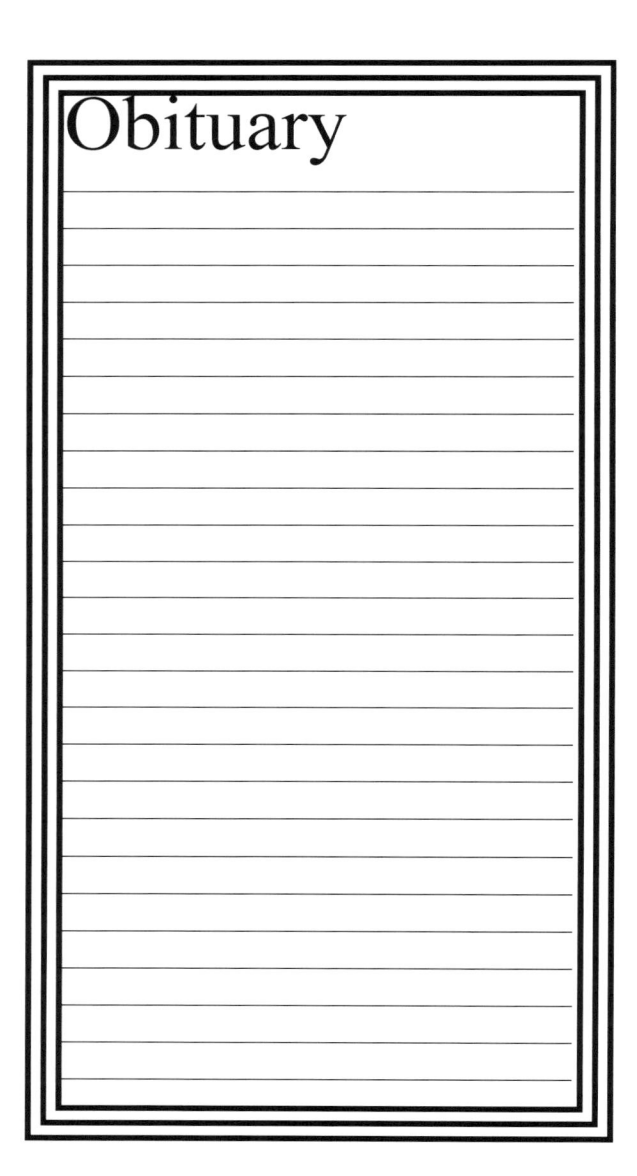

Obituary

Weddings

Creative Writing Activity: Dream or Nightmare: Student will write a dream or nightmare one of the characters in the story may have, and illustrate it.

Writing Skills Activity: Student will use this form or write in their notebook.

Point of View: Point of View is telling a story from one person's view. Student will write about an event in this story from a different character's point of view.

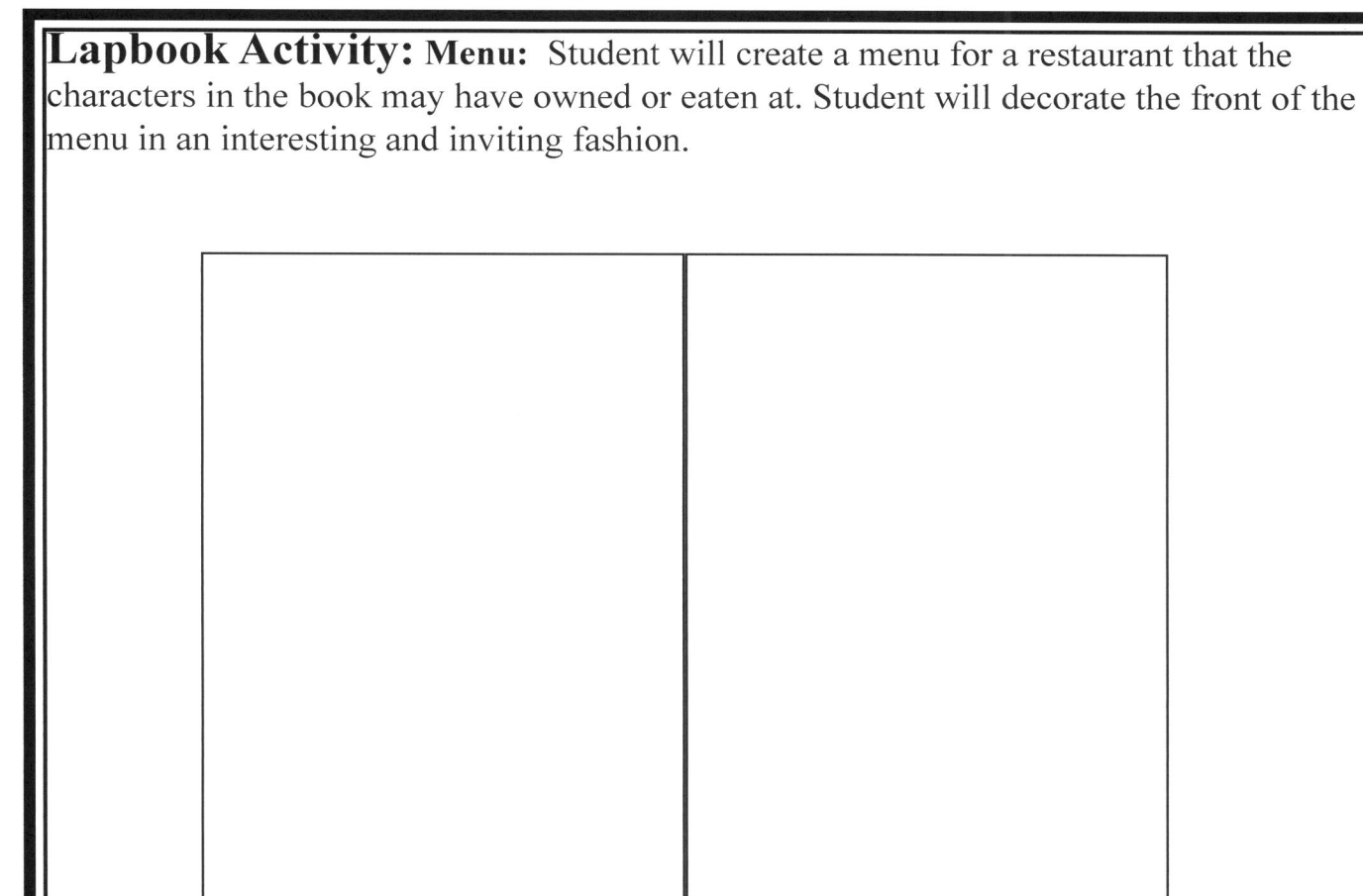

Lapbook Activity: Menu: Student will create a menu for a restaurant that the characters in the book may have owned or eaten at. Student will decorate the front of the menu in an interesting and inviting fashion.

Poster Board Activity:
Chalk Art
On a black poster board student will use colored chalk to illustrate a scene or event in the story.

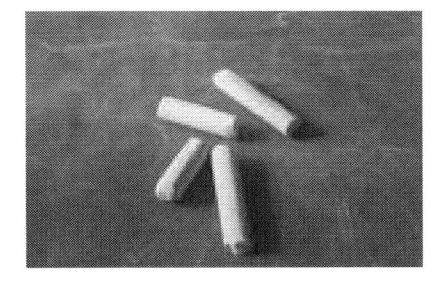

Creative Art Activity:
Paper Doll
Student will cut out pictures from the internet of people to represent the characters in this story and then laminate them and glue them onto sticks. Students can use them to act out parts of the story or the dialogue the student wrote in an earlier lesson.

Lesson 7
Activities

Lesson 7 Activities: Students will use the book they are studying and information found on the internet for the following activities. Then the student will write the information required for this activity on the patterns or in their notebook. The patterns may be cut out and placed on the lapbook.

Encyclopedia:
Student will choose one subject from this lesson that interested them and look it up on the internet or in encyclopedia. They will write the name of the subject across the top of the monitor pattern. On the monitor screen section, they will write three or more interesting facts about the subject.

Journal:
Student will imagine that they are one of the characters from the story. After reading each lesson, they will write a short journal entry telling what happened from that character's point of view.
Student will also draw a picture to go along with the journal entry.
At the end of the book, student will staple all the journal entries together to form a complete booklet.
They can even create a special cover for it from construction paper.

Vocabulary word: _____
Definition of the word: _____
_____
_____

Antonym of the word: _____
How many syllables does the word have? _____

Vocabulary Word: _____
Sentence using the word: _____
_____
_____

Synonym of the word: _____

Vocabulary: Student will use the vocabulary words from the list for this lesson. On one of the patterns, or on one index card they will write one vocabulary word. They should also write the definition of the word, then the Antonym and how many Syllables the word has.

On the other card, the student will write the same word. They will write a full sentence using this word and then write the Synonym of the word.

They will repeat this for all the vocabulary words in this lesson.

Place the patterns or cards in an envelope which can be glued into the student's notebook or onto the lapbook..

Sequencing: At the end of the lesson the student will write two of the main events on these two strips. Save them in an envelope which can be glued onto the lapbook or in the notebook. At the end of the book, these strips can be taken out and the student can arrange them in the correct order as they occurred in the story.

Handwriting: Student will pick their favorite sentence that they read in this lesson. Have them write the sentence in their best handwriting on this page or in their notebook.

Student will write out the answers for the following:

Main Idea: In a sentence or two, write what the main idea was of this section.

Key Event: In a sentence or two write what the most important event was in this section.

Prediction: In a sentence of two write what you Predict will happen in the next section.

Comparison: In a sentence of two compare two things in this section. Tell what makes them alike and what makes them different.

Fact or Opinion: In one sentence write a fact about this section and one sentence that is an opinion about the lesson.

Cause and Effect: When one thing happens in a story, many other things happen because of this one event. This is called cause and effect. In the center circle, student will write one thing that happened in the story (the cause). In the smaller circles, student will write the variety of things that happened because of that main cause (the effects).

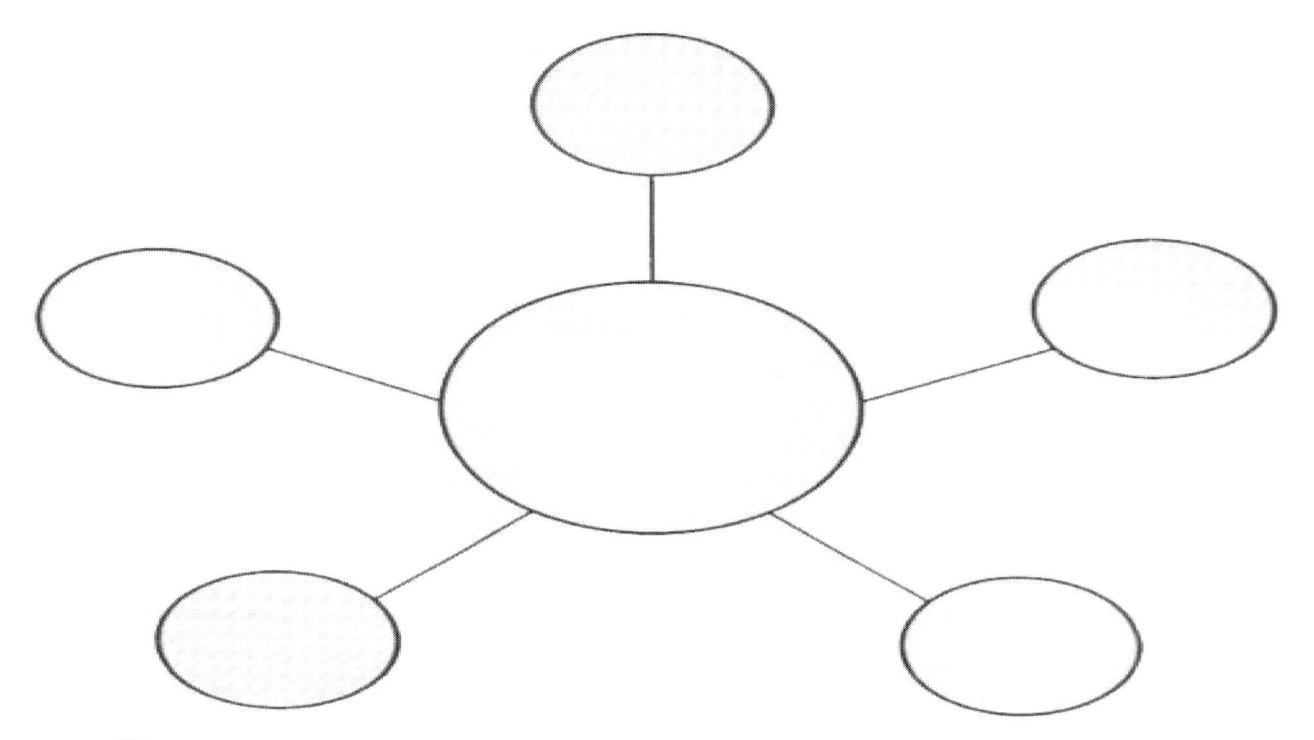

Poetry Form: Student will write a poem about the book or characters using this format.

Tanka: A Tanka is a form of Japanese poetry that depends on the number of lines and syllables instead of rhyme. The pattern is:
Line 1 = 5 syllables, Line 2 = 7 syllables
Line 3 = 5 syllables, Line 4 = 7 syllables
Line 5 = 7 syllables

Example:
  Blue-eyed baby cubs
  wobble out of winter's den
  warm sun on cold fur
  forest smells of fresh, cold pine
  wild, new world to grow into.

Newspaper Activity: Student will use this form to write their newspaper piece on then paste it onto their newspaper lay out poster.

Society News Section: Student will write about someone in the story who would be considered a fairly famous person or character. Write a society column about an event or party that they may have attended.

Society News

Creative Writing Activity: Tall Tales: Tall tales are humorous, exaggerated stories common on the American frontier. Student will write a tall tale about one of the characters in the story and then illustrate it.

Writing Skills Activity: Student will use this form or write in their notebook.

Compare and Contrast: Compare and Contrast tell about two or more things and how they are alike or different. Student will write to Compare and Contrast two characters in the story.

Writing Skills Activity: Student will use this form or write in their notebook.

Lapbook Activity: Fashion Designer: Student will design clothing that one or more of the characters in the story would have worn. Student will color them or cut them out of scraps of material and put them on the doll form that represents the character and then attach to lapbook.

Poster Board Activity:
Silhouette
Using black construction paper, student will cut out a silhouette of the main character or an item from the story and glue it onto the center of a white or colored 1/2 poster board. Then student will create a frame around the outside with a black poster board.

Creative Art Activity:
Book Mark
Using thick tag board, student will cut into a rectangle 3 inches by 6 inches, and create a book mark that resembles something about the book. Then student will punch a hole in the end and tie ribbon or string through it. Laminate it if possible.

Lesson 8
Activities

Lesson 8 Activities: Students will use the book they are studying and information found on the internet for the following activities. Then the student will write the information required for this activity on the patterns or in their notebook. The patterns may be cut out and placed on the lapbook.

Encyclopedia:
Student will choose one subject from this lesson that interested them and look it up on the internet or in encyclopedia. They will write the name of the subject across the top of the monitor pattern. On the monitor screen section, they will write three or more interesting facts about the subject.

Journal:
Student will imagine that they are one of the characters from the story. After reading each lesson, they will write a short journal entry telling what happened from that character's point of view.
Student will also draw a picture to go along with the journal entry.
At the end of the book, student will staple all the journal entries together to form a complete booklet.
They can even create a special cover for it from construction paper.

Vocabulary word: _____
Definition of the word: _____
_____
_____

Antonym of the word: _____
How many syllables does the word have? _____

Vocabulary Word: _____
Sentence using the word: _____
_____
_____

Synonym of the word: _____

Vocabulary: Student will use the vocabulary words from the list for this lesson. On one of the patterns, or on one index card they will write one vocabulary word. They should also write the definition of the word, then the Antonym and how many Syllables the word has.

On the other card, the student will write the same word. They will write a full sentence using this word and then write the Synonym of the word.

They will repeat this for all the vocabulary words in this lesson.

Place the patterns or cards in an envelope which can be glued into the student's notebook or onto the lapbook..

Sequencing: At the end of the lesson the student will write two of the main events on these two strips. Save them in an envelope which can be glued onto the lapbook or in the notebook. At the end of the book, these strips can be taken out and the student can arrange them in the correct order as they occurred in the story.

Handwriting: Student will pick their favorite sentence that they read in this lesson. Have them write the sentence in their best handwriting on this page or in their notebook.

Student will write out the answers for the following:
Main Idea: In a sentence or two, write what the main idea was of this section.
___

Key Event: In a sentence or two write what the most important event was in this section.
___

Prediction: In a sentence of two write what you Predict will happen in the next section.
___

Comparison: In a sentence of two compare two things in this section. Tell what makes them alike and what makes them different.
___

Fact or Opinion: In one sentence write a fact about this section and one sentence that is an opinion about the lesson.
___

Descriptions: Authors use descriptive words so that the reader can imagine the place or thing that is being described. Student will find one place in the book that the author really described well and write the name of the place inside the polygon. On the lines coming out of the polygon, student will write the words the author used to describe the place such as pretty, dark, blue....

Poetry Form: Student will write a poem about the book or characters using this format.

Diamanté: A diamanté is a seven-line, diamond-shaped poem which contrasts two opposites. The pattern is: First Line and seventh line - Name the opposites. Second and sixth lines - Two adjectives describing the opposite nearest it. Third and fifth lines - Three participles (ing words) describing the nearest opposite.
Fourth line - two nouns for each of the opposites.

Example:	Fish
	silvered, baited
	teeming, swimming, darting
	scaled amphibian, graceful hind
	running, leaping, grazing
	hunted, mammal
	Deer

Newspaper Activity: Student will use this form to write their newspaper piece on then paste it onto their newspaper lay out poster.

Sports Section: Student will imagine that one of the characters in your book is in a sports competition and write a newspaper article about it and then illustrate it as well.

Sports

Creative Writing Activity: **Memoir:** When writing a memoir, a person chooses one time or one event and expounds upon it by stretching the truth. Student will write a memoir as if they were a character in the story. They should choose one event to write about, and stretch the truth in the retelling.

My Memoir

Writing Skills Activity: Student will use this form or write in their notebook.

Sequel: A sequel is a movie or book that follows another. The sequel contains the same characters and follows the same story line. The characters and story line may change during the sequel but they have to start out the same to show the connection with the previous story. Students will write the first few paragraphs of a sequel for this story.

Lapbook Activity: Book Cover Puzzle: Student will glue a picture they print from the internet of the book cover, onto this puzzle pattern so that the pattern shows on the back. Then student will cut the book cover into puzzle pieces. This can go in an envelope on the lapbook to be put together later.

Poster Board Activity:
Board Game
Student will create a board game on the poster board to use with this story.

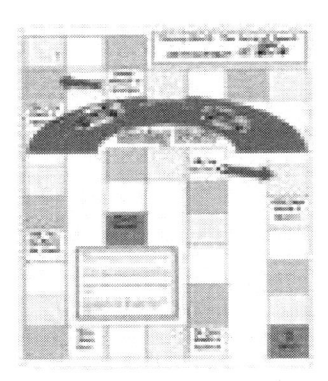

Creative Art Activity:
Photography
Photography is a great form of art. Student will find things that reminds them of this book and take some photos of it. Get these printed in black and white and some in color. Student can turn these into cards, frame them or take photos of one item in different angles and create a unique photo like this one.

Lesson 9
Activity

Lesson 9 Activities: Students will use the book they are studying and information found on the internet for the following activities. Then the student will write the information required for this activity on the patterns or in their notebook. The patterns may be cut out and placed on the lapbook.

Encyclopedia:
Student will choose one subject from this lesson that interested them and look it up on the internet or in encyclopedia. They will write the name of the subject across the top of the monitor pattern. On the monitor screen section, they will write three or more interesting facts about the subject.

Journal:
Student will imagine that they are one of the characters from the story. After reading each lesson, they will write a short journal entry telling what happened from that character's point of view.
Student will also draw a picture to go along with the journal entry.
At the end of the book, student will staple all the journal entries together to form a complete booklet.
They can even create a special cover for it from construction paper.

Vocabulary word: _____
Definition of the word: _____
_____
_____

Antonym of the word: _____
How many syllables does the word have? _____

Vocabulary Word: _____
Sentence using the word: _____
_____
_____

Synonym of the word: _____

Vocabulary: Student will use the vocabulary words from the list for this lesson. On one of the patterns, or on one index card they will write one vocabulary word. They should also write the definition of the word, then the Antonym and how many Syllables the word has.

On the other card, the student will write the same word. They will write a full sentence using this word and then write the Synonym of the word.

They will repeat this for all the vocabulary words in this lesson.

Place the patterns or cards in an envelope which can be glued into the student's notebook or onto the lapbook..

Sequencing: At the end of the lesson the student will write two of the main events on these two strips. Save them in an envelope which can be glued onto the lapbook or in the notebook. At the end of the book, these strips can be taken out and the student can arrange them in the correct order as they occurred in the story.

Handwriting: Student will pick their favorite sentence that they read in this lesson. Have them write the sentence in their best handwriting on this page or in their notebook.

Student will write out the answers for the following:
Main Idea: In a sentence or two, write what the main idea was of this section.
_____
_____
_____
_____
_____
_____

Key Event: In a sentence or two write what the most important event was in this section.
_____
_____
_____
_____
_____
_____

Prediction: In a sentence of two write what you Predict will happen in the next section.
_____
_____
_____
_____
_____
_____

Comparison: In a sentence of two compare two things in this section. Tell what makes them alike and what makes them different.
_____
_____
_____
_____
_____

Fact or Opinion: In one sentence write a fact about this section and one sentence that is an opinion about the lesson.
_____
_____
_____
_____
_____
_____

Pyramid of Importance: Each character in the story holds a position of importance. Some are of main importance, some are of less importance. Student will fill in the pyramid with the names of the characters. The top should have the most important character, the next line the next most important characters and continue down until you have listed all the characters in order of importance.

Poetry Form: Student will write a poem about the book or characters using this format.

Lantern: A lantern is a five line poem in the shape of a Japanese lantern. The Pattern is:
Line 1: noun (one syllable)
Line 2: describe the noun (two syllables)
Line 3: describe the noun (three syllables
Line 4: describe the noun (four syllables)
Line 5: Synonym for noun in line one (one syllable)

Example:	Mane
	long, thick
	blonde to black
	royal mantle
	Fur

Newspaper Activity: Student will use this form to write their newspaper piece on then paste it onto their newspaper lay out poster.

Entertainment Section: Book Review Student will write an over all review of the book and tell what they liked and did not like, which characters seemed real and which scenes were described the best. Student should also ad a picture of the book cover.

Book Review

Creative Writing Activity: Newberry Award:
Each year one book is chosen to receive the John Newberry Award for great writing. Student will write a short report on why this book did or should have won the award.

Writing Skills Activity: Student will use this form or write in their notebook.

Climax: The climax of a story is the point where the reader knows who wins the conflict or how the problem will be solved. Student will write what the main problem was and at what point they knew how it would be solved.

Writing Skills Activity: Student will use this form or write in their notebook.

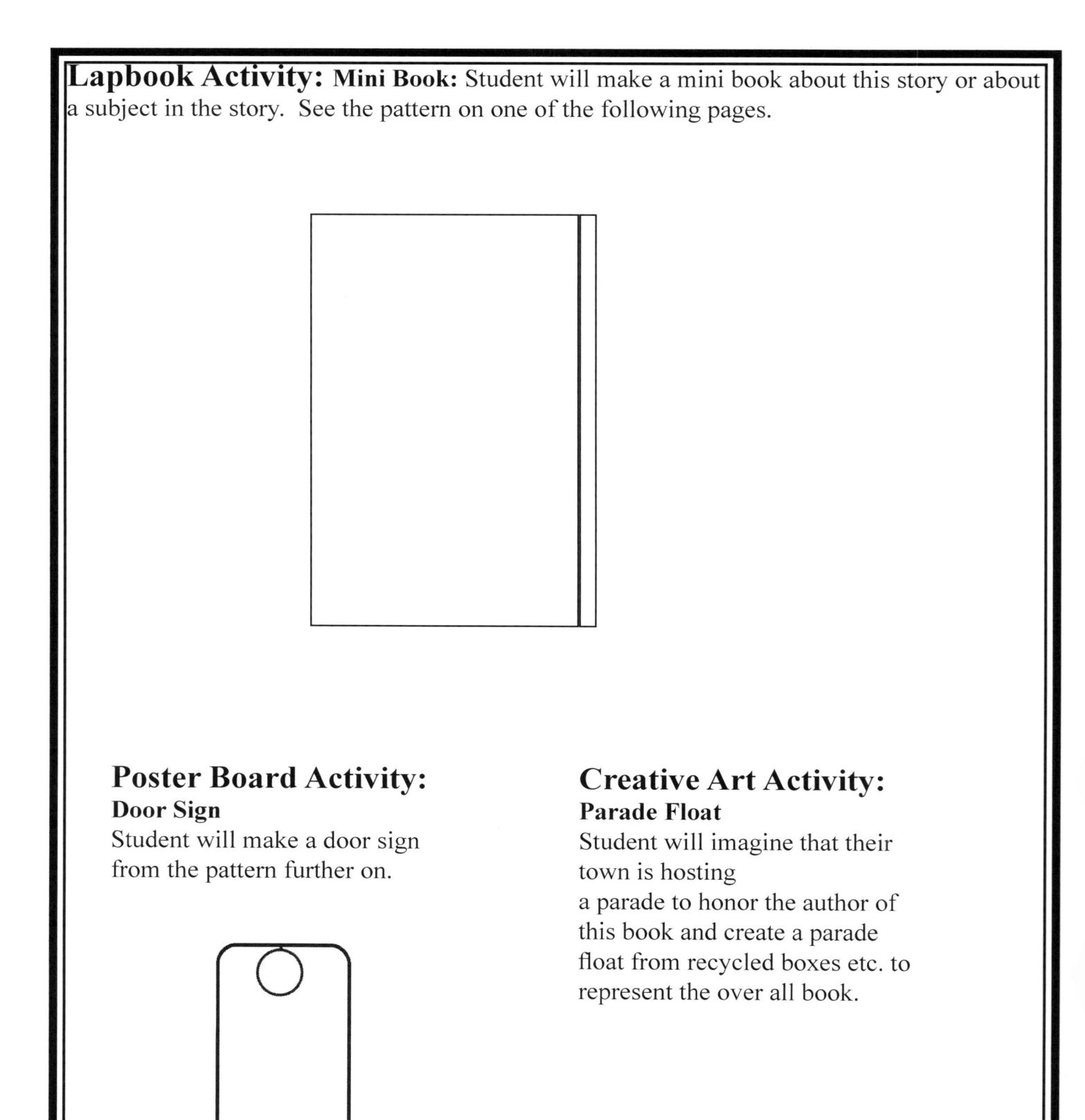

Lapbook Activity: Mini Book: Student will make a mini book about this story or about a subject in the story. See the pattern on one of the following pages.

Poster Board Activity:
Door Sign
Student will make a door sign from the pattern further on.

Creative Art Activity:
Parade Float
Student will imagine that their town is hosting a parade to honor the author of this book and create a parade float from recycled boxes etc. to represent the over all book.

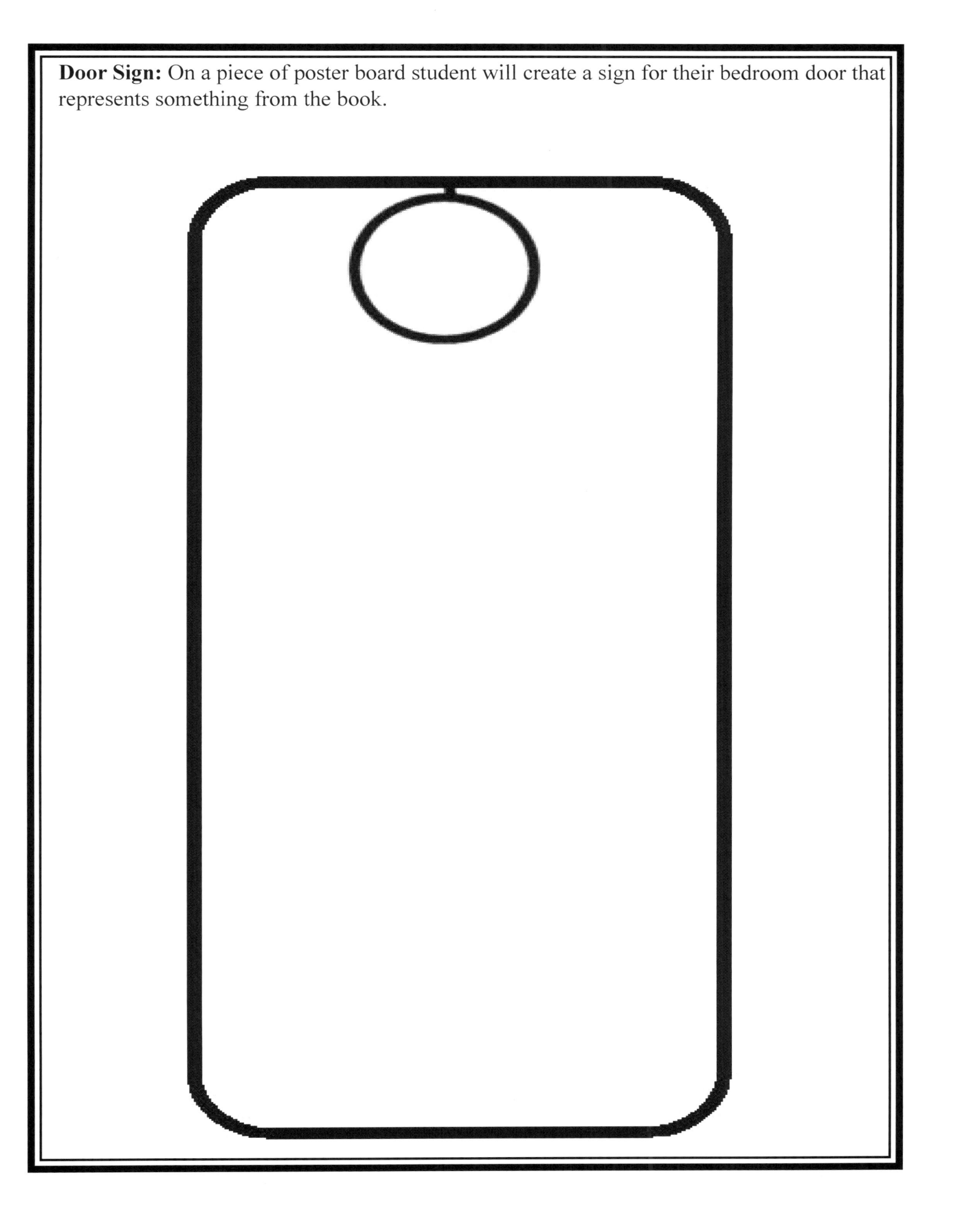

Door Sign: On a piece of poster board student will create a sign for their bedroom door that represents something from the book.

Mini Book : Student will create a mini book that retells the story. This may be put on the Lapbook.

2　　　　　　　　　　　　　　　　　　　　　　　　　　　　　　　　　11

Print double sided. Cut on the red lines. Fold on the dotted lines.

10 | 3

8 | 5

Print double sided. Cut on the red lines. Fold on the dotted lines.

4 | 9

6 | 7

Lesson 10
Activities

Lesson 10 Activities: Students will use the book they are studying and information found on the internet for the following activities. Then the student will write the information required for this activity on the patterns or in their notebook. The patterns may be cut out and placed on the lapbook.

Encyclopedia:
Student will choose one subject from this lesson that interested them and look it up on the internet or in encyclopedia. They will write the name of the subject across the top of the monitor pattern. On the monitor screen section, they will write three or more interesting facts about the subject.

Journal:
Student will imagine that they are one of the characters from the story. After reading each lesson, they will write a short journal entry telling what happened from that character's point of view.
Student will also draw a picture to go along with the journal entry.
At the end of the book, student will staple all the journal entries together to form a complete booklet.
They can even create a special cover for it from construction paper.

Vocabulary word: _____
Definition of the word: _____
_____
_____

Antonym of the word: _____
How many syllables does the word have? _____

Vocabulary Word: _____
Sentence using the word: _____
_____
_____

Synonym of the word: _____

_____
_____
_____
_____
_____
_____

Vocabulary: Student will use the vocabulary words from the list for this lesson. On one of the patterns, or on one index card they will write one vocabulary word. They should also write the definition of the word, then the Antonym and how many Syllables the word has.

On the other card, the student will write the same word. They will write a full sentence using this word and then write the Synonym of the word.

They will repeat this for all the vocabulary words in this lesson.

Place the patterns or cards in an envelope which can be glued into the student's notebook or onto the lapbook..

Sequencing: At the end of the lesson the student will write two of the main events on these two strips. Save them in an envelope which can be glued onto the lapbook or in the notebook. At the end of the book, these strips can be taken out and the student can arrange them in the correct order as they occurred in the story.

Handwriting: Student will pick their favorite sentence that they read in this lesson. Have them write the sentence in their best handwriting on this page or in their notebook.

Student will write out the answers for the following:
Main Idea: In a sentence or two, write what the main idea was of this section.

Key Event: In a sentence or two write what the most important event was in this section.

Prediction: In a sentence of two write what you Predict will happen in the next section.

Comparison: In a sentence of two compare two things in this section. Tell what makes them alike and what makes them different.

Fact or Opinion: In one sentence write a fact about this section and one sentence that is an opinion about the lesson.

Hero vs. Villain: Most stories usually have a hero (the main character) and a villain. The villain may not seem that bad. The villain is usually the character who stands in the way of the main character, or against the main character. Student will name the Hero and the Villain and fill in the "What the Villain does...." square.

What the Villain does to hinder the Hero.

Hero

Villain

Poetry Form: Student will write a poem about the book or characters using this format.

Shape Poem: To be done on a separate sheet of paper. Shape poems can be made by placing words, which describe a particular object, in such a way that they form the shape of the object. Student will start by making a simple outline of the shape or object (an animal, a football, a fruit etc.) large enough to fill a piece of paper. Then student will brainstorm a minimum of ten words and phrases that describe the shape including action and feeling words as well. Next, student will place a piece of paper over the shape and decide where the words are going to be placed so that they outline the shape but also fit well together. Separate words and phrases with commas. Shape poems can also be created by simply filling in the shape with a poem, as well.

Newspaper Activity: Student will use this form to write their newspaper piece on then paste it onto their newspaper lay out poster.

Word Search Section: Find all the words

```
X J D U R A I L U C E P C Y E
S S E N S U O I C S N O C L M
P P B F R D E K N K N Y O G B
E E I O E E T E D C L L N N A
C R R L D S T E S S I S I R
U M C T U N A N S B T B P T R
L I S U C A T E S A N E I A A
A S E N T R L S E S E R C E S
T S R A A T U R R E M A U S S
I I P T N S T O P M E T O U I
O O I E T E U W M E L E U A N
N N L L R V I U I N E D S N G
G E H Y P O C R I T I C A L U
R S D E D N I M T N E S B A T
S P O R A D I C A L L Y K Q S
```

**ABSENTMINDED BASEMENT CONCENTRATING
CONSCIOUSNESS CONSPICUOUS ELEMENTS
EMBARRASSING GUTS HYPOCRITICAL
IMPRESSED LIBERATED NAUSEATINGLY
PECULIAR PERMISSION PRESCRIBED
RELENTLESSLY RELUCTANT RETREATING
SENSE SPECULATION SPORADICALLY
STRANDED TASTE UNFORTUNATELY
WORSE**

Creative Writing Activity: A Different End: Student will write a different ending for the story.

Writing Skills Activity: Plot Analysis Board
Student will create this by following the directions.

What you need:
Index Cards, Pictures from the internet, Markers, Crayons. Glue

1. Fold the poster board in half so that it makes a folder.
2. Decorate the front of the folder with pictures and information that includes the Title, the Author, the Illustrator, and the Publisher.
3. On index cards, write the information requested below. Glue the index cards inside the folder. You can put pictures on the cards to go along with them.

   Information to put on cards:
   1. Main Character and Character Traits
   2. Main Setting
   3. Other Characters
   4. Other Settings in the Story
   5. Main Problem
   6. Other Problems
   7. Climax
   8. Solution to the Problem
   9. Your favorite part of the story
   10. What you would change if you could about the story.

Lapbook Activity: The Commandments:
Student will cut out the patter and fold so that the Ten Commandments are on the front. Inside student will write how a character may have broken or upheld one or more of these commandments. Attach to Lapbook.

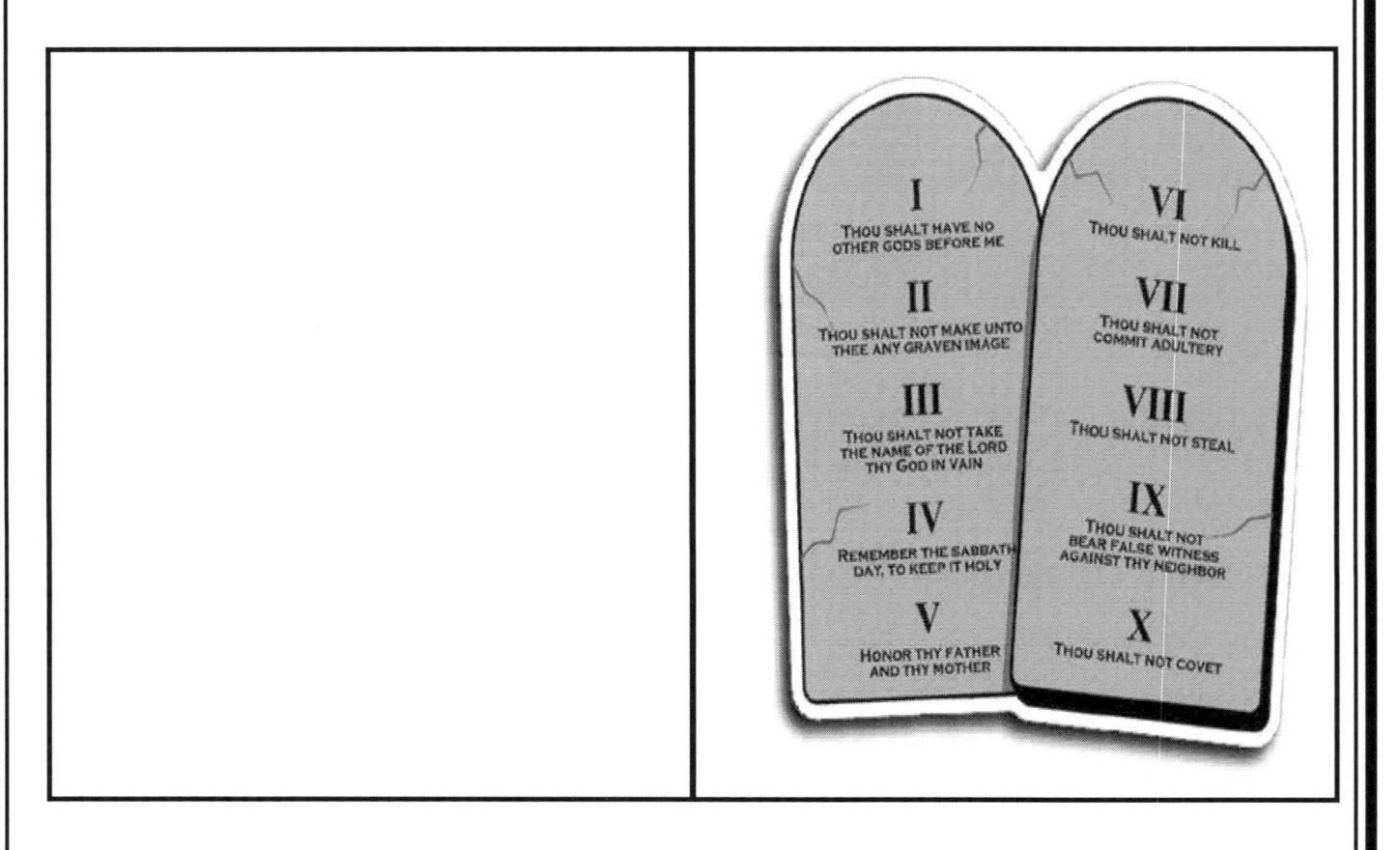

I Thou shalt have no other gods before me
II Thou shalt not make unto thee any graven image
III Thou shalt not take the name of the Lord thy God in vain
IV Remember the Sabbath day, to keep it holy
V Honor thy father and thy mother
VI Thou shalt not kill
VII Thou shalt not commit adultery
VIII Thou shalt not steal
IX Thou shalt not bear false witness against thy neighbor
X Thou shalt not covet

Poster Board Activity:
Jeopardy
On the poster board student will create a game board like the one on the next page. They will cut out several sets of the play money. The teacher will write 4 to 8 questions for each category. The student then picks one category and the dollar amount of the question they will try and answer. The teacher or student reads the question. If the answer is correct the student wins the amount of money that they chose. The next player takes a turn. The winner is the one with the most

Creative Art Activity:
Sketch
Student will imagine they are a sketch artist and using black pencils or charcoal pencils, they will sketch some of the main characters, places or events from the story.

JEOPARDY

People	Places	Animals	Other
$100	$100	$100	$100
$200	$200	$200	$200
$300	$300	$300	$300
$400	$400	$400	$400

1
ONE
ONE DOLLAR
5
FIVE
10
TEN
20
TWENTY
100
HUNDRED
1
ONE
ONE DOLLAR
5
FIVE
10
TEN
20
TWENTY

Additional Activities

Additional Writing Activities

Imaginative: Imaginative writing is when you write a fanciful story using your imagination. Student will write one that comes to mind while they read this book.

Essay: An essay is a short piece of writing, from an author's personal point of view. Student will write a short essay from their point of view about a subject that comes to mind while reading these books.

Speech: A speech is the act of delivering a formal spoken communication to an audience . Student will write a short speech that one of the characters from the books may have given.

Autobiography: An autobiography is a story of a person's life. Student will write a short autobiography outline of one of the characters or they could write about the author as well.

Humor: Humor allows the reader to laugh and enjoy a story. Student will write a humorous piece about a subject or thing mentioned in these books.

ABC Story: ABC Stories are short stories that have each sentence starting with the next letter in the alphabet. Student will write a short ABC story about an event or one of the characters in the book. For example:
 A girl named Kit lived in America. By noon she was happy...

Literature Web: A story will make you think of many things and feel many things. Student will draw this chart in their notebook and fill it in.

Key Words: What were some important words or phrases?

Feelings: What feelings did you have while reading the book?

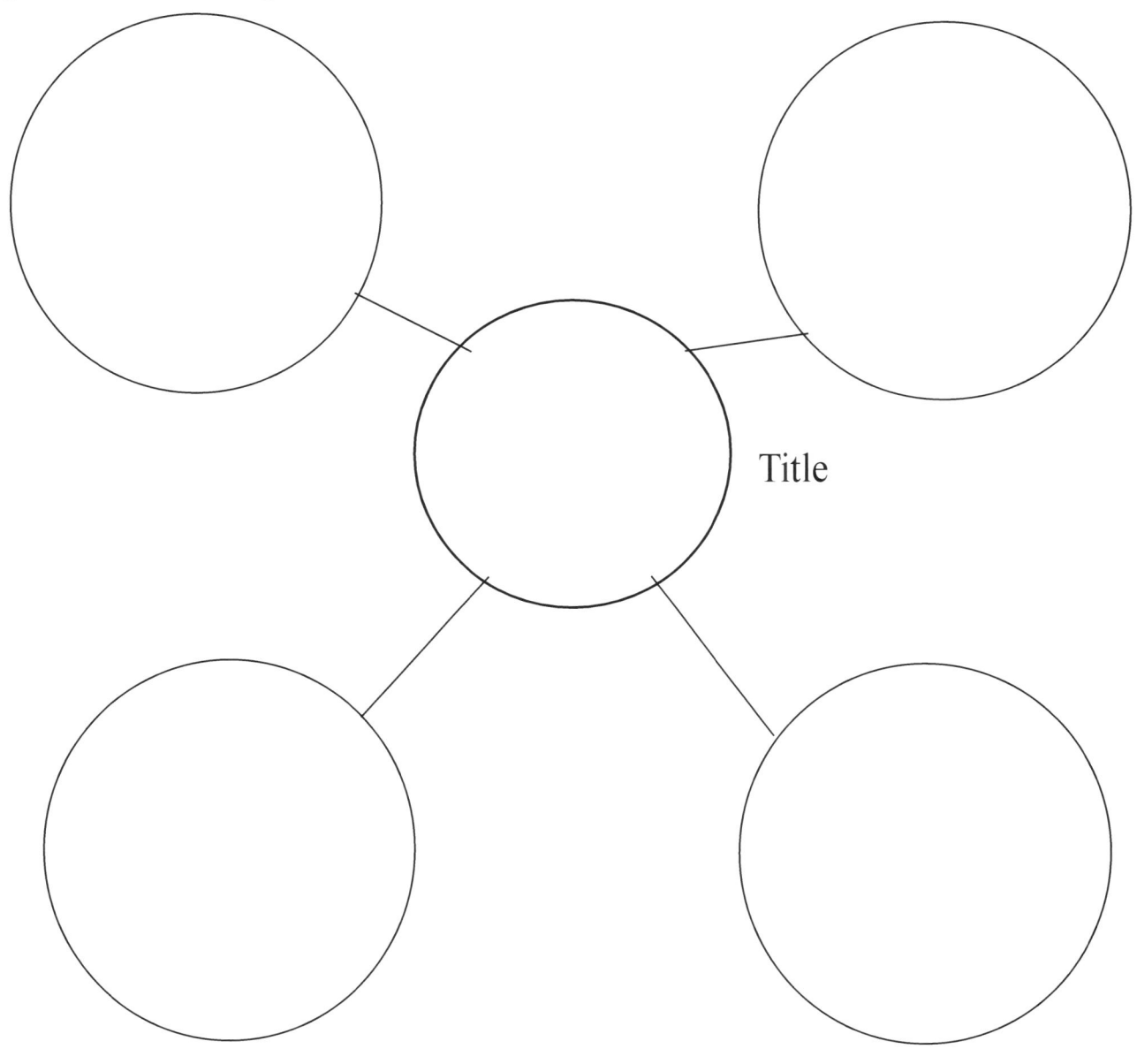

Title

Symbols: Did the author use any symbols in the story?

Attitude: What do you think the authors attitude is about the subject this story is about?

Sign Language:
On a piece of poster board, student will glue a larger versions of the sign language alphabet. Now the teacher will sign a name, scene or vocabulary word from the story. Students try to figure the word out by pointing to the correct sign language letter and spelling out the words.

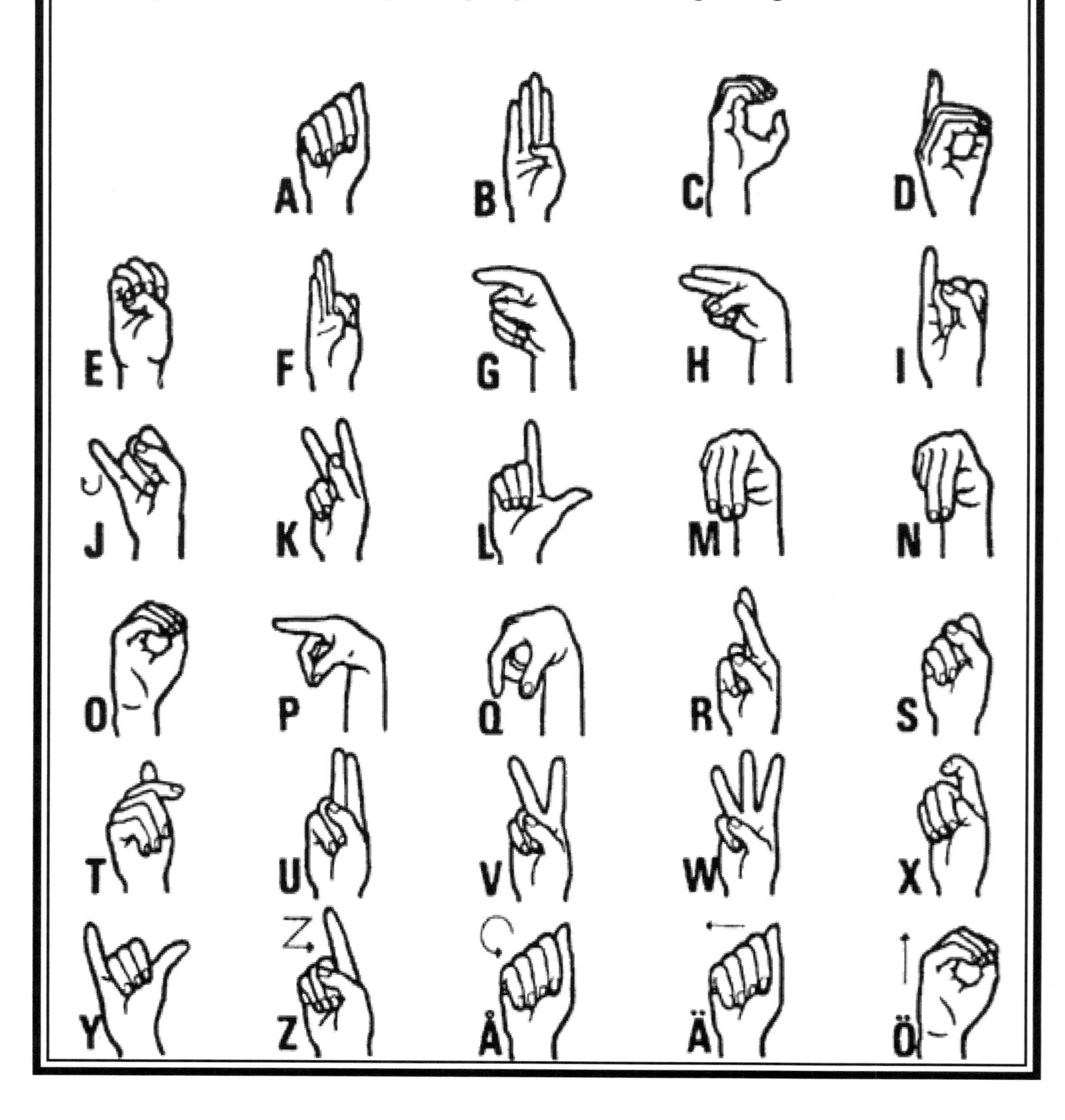

Theater Box:

Get a cardboard box with a flat side larger than a piece of paper. In the side cut out a square about 6 by 9 inches. This will be the opening for your theater.

While reading each chapter of the book, Student will draw one or more of the main scenes on 8 1/2 by 11 inch drawing paper. Stay within the inner 6 by 9 inches though. Color these with markers, paint, colored pencils etc.

Figure out a way that these pictures can be slid in and out of the box, so they appear in the opening and it looks like you are changing scenes, or draw them all on one long roll, and create rollers in each end of the box out of paper towel rolls.

At the end of the book you should have a whole story in these scenes. Present the scenes in your theater to family or friends. You will have to act as the announcer and explain the main events in each scene.

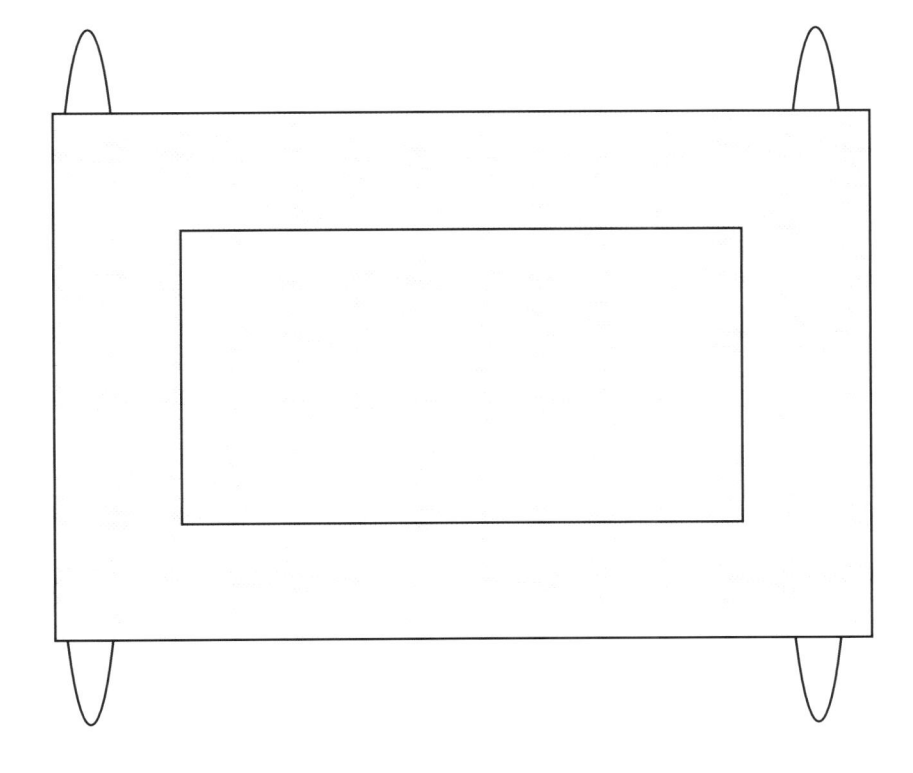

Acting: Student will

1. Dress up as one of the characters in the story. They can act out their favorite part of the story.
2. Host a talk show where another member of the family acts as the television host. Your student is the main character of the story. They ask you questions about the story.
3. Hold a trial. Someone dresses up as the villain in the story. Someone dresses up as the main character. Someone as a lawyer and someone as a judge. Hold a trial to determine if the villain is really guilty of crimes or not.

Rock Art:
Student will gather smooth rocks of different shapes and sizes. Student will clean the rocks and when dry create characters from the book with the rocks, by painting them, making clothes for them and gluing on google eyes.

Name Art:
Student will write the main characters name in the middle of 1/4 poster board and then decorate all around it in any art form they like.

Carving:

Use soap or wax and carve a character from the story. All you need to carve soap is a bar of soap and a spoon. If your child is old enough to use a butter knife then you can let them have a butter knife to carve their soap with. Soap carving can be messy so it is best to be done on a table covered with an old cloth or newspaper. And everyone doing the carving should have old clothes on.

When carving soap, you can use any size bar of soap you would like, but a nice big bar of soap is better to get creative with. If you are lucky enough to have a bar of home made lye soap that will work as well. Unwrap your bar of soap and decide what you want to make with your bar of soap. Soap is a soft material so a spoon will work to carve a bar of soap just fine. A knife can give your bar of soap more detail then a spoon can but it is more dangerous.

Sewing:

Use felt and material stuffing. Create a pattern for something from the story such as an animal or character. Cut out two of the same patterns from the felt. Have student sew around the outside edges. Stuff with stuffing and complete the sewing.

Design a Needlepoint:
Get graph paper and have student design a needlepoint by placing an x in the boxes to design the picture.

Shape Puzzle: On poster board student will draw out a large copy of the shape of a character or item from the book. Cut it into a puzzle pattern.

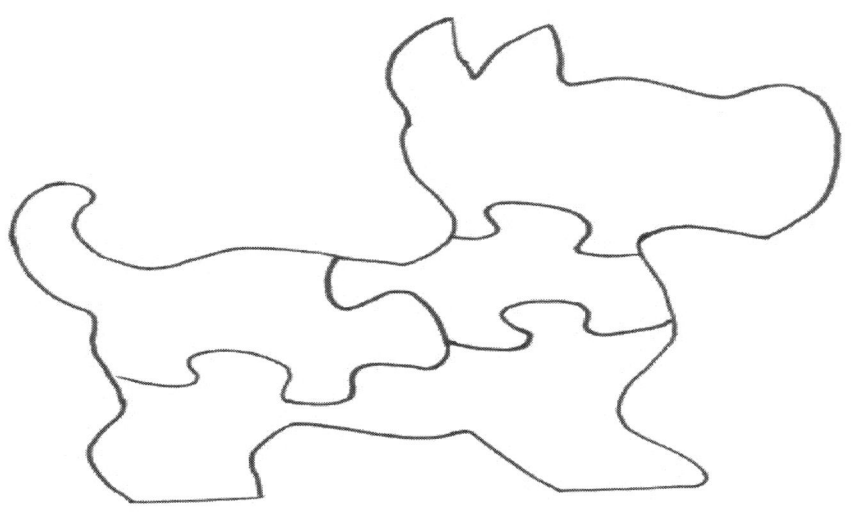

I Spy

Student will find pictures on the internet of things that come to mind while reading this book. Pictures of the characters, of the vocabulary words etc. Student will print and then glue them all over the poster board. Now they should make an I spy set of calling cards on index cards.

For example your cards would say:

I spy a cat.

I spy a rat.

Give the cards to a younger child and see if they can find all the items on the I spy poster.

Bingo: Print as many of these Bingo boards as you need for the students. Write the vocabulary words in the squares of the Bingo boards. Each board should be different. Use the definition index cards as the call cards for the game.

B	I	N	G	O
		Free Space		

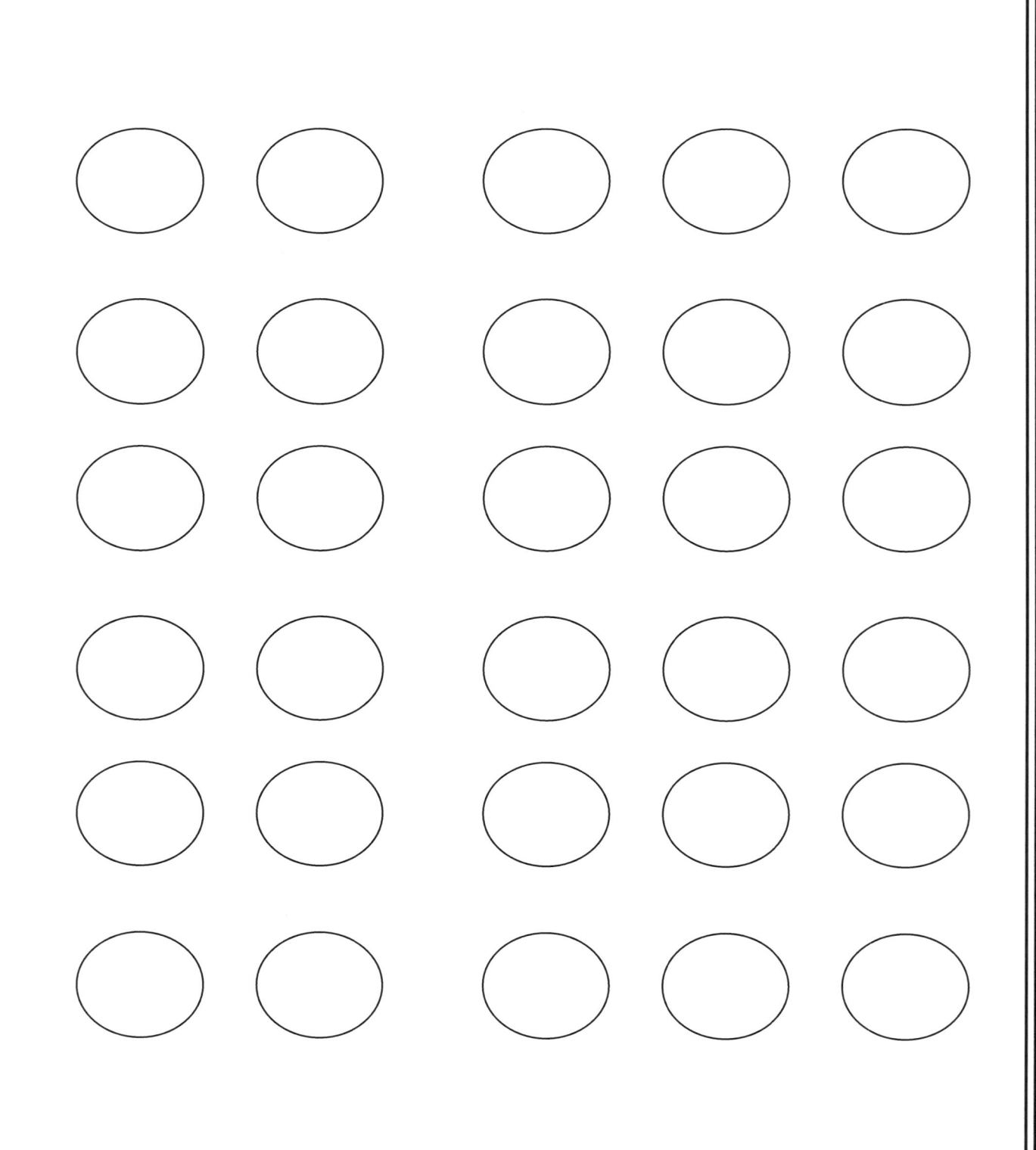

Comprehension

The following pages have the
Fill in the Blanks,
True and False,
Multiple Choice
and
Who, What, Where, When,
Why and How Questions
for all lessons.

Use the Vocabulary words
on the following page for the
questions

Lesson 1	Chapters 1-2
Lesson 2	Chapters 3
Lesson 3	Chapters 4
Lesson 4	Chapters 5
Lesson 5	Chapters 6
Lesson 6	Chapters 7-8
Lesson 7	Chapters 9
Lesson 8	Chapters 10
Lesson 9	Chapters 11
Lesson 10	Chapters 12-13

Vocabulary Words:

Lesson 1. figured pandemonium cuds taste bragger grits peculiar nauseatingly hypocritical proverbial.

Lesson 2. reaction basement retreating inherited embarrassing sarcasm snottiest repulsive drought conspicuous.

Lesson 3. devoted territory melodic worse consolation prissily rumpus impressed contempt ominously.

Lesson 4. unfortunately revenge tangle council suspended shuffling deserves spreading prideful punctuation.

Lesson 5. obsessed speculation sense foundling paralyzed prescribed imitated guardian noble jester.

Lesson 6. absentminded reluctant nuisance encounter obliged complacent trick spectacle bargaining tantrum.

Lesson 7. perceive elements conspiring peculiar concentrating arise dignity sporadically hesitate vanquished.

Lesson 8. scrawny genuine anxiety guts permission absorbed sacred drunk liberated protest.

Lesson 9. relentlessly numbness consciousness dreadful apologize threatened nightmare sensation accusation doused

LESSON 1
FILL IN THE BLANKS / COMPREHENSION
Write the word to complete the sentence. / Write a full sentence to answer the questions.

Vocabulary: cuds   taste   figured   grits   peculiar

1. He _____ if he worked at it, he could be the fastest runner in the fifth grade.
2. It had put into his mouth a _____ for running.
3. The cows in the field were lazily chewing their _____.
4. These _____ are scorching the bottom of the pot.
5. He thought how _____ it was, that was the biggest thing in his life.

MULTIPLE CHOICE / TRUE AND FALSE
Write the letter for the best answer. / Write T for true and F for false.

1. _____ How many sisters does Jesse have?
   A. 4   B. 2
   C. 5   D. 1
2. _____ What is the name of Jesse's school?
   A. Ben Franklin Elementary   B. Abe Lincoln Elementary
   C. Lark Creek Elementary   D. George Washington Elementary
3. _____ Who was Miss Bessie?
   A. the dog   B. Jesse's teacher
   C. the cat   D. the milk cow
4. _____ What is Jesse's nick-name?
   A. Runner Boy   B. Jess
   C. Oliver   D. Lazy Boy

1. _____ Jess liked to draw, he loved it.

2. _____ Leslie Burke was a boy about Jesse's age

3. _____ Jess was in love with the music teacher, Miss Edmunds.

4. _____ The new neighbors did not have any children.

Lesson 1
Write full sentences for this section:

1. Who moved into the Perkins place?
2. What did Jess practice everyday?
3. Where did Jess practice running?
4. When Jess drew, what did he draw?
5. Why did he run everyday?
6. How did Jess draw his crazy animals?

(Who) _____
_____
_____
_____

(What) _____
_____
_____
_____

(Where) _____
_____
_____
_____

(When) _____
_____
_____
_____

(Why) _____
_____
_____
_____

(How) _____
_____
_____
_____

LESSON 2
FILL IN THE BLANKS / COMPREHENSION
Write the word to complete the sentence. / Write a full sentence to answer the questions.

Words: snottiest   retreating   repulsive   reaction   sarcasm

1. The _____ didn't seem to bother her.
2. She swung a pointed glance at Mr. Turner's _____ form.
3. Mary Lou was at work being the second _____ girl in the fifth grade.
4. That smell is very_____.
5. Next thing, his voice dripping with _____, you're going to let some girl run.

MULTIPLE CHOICE / TRUE AND FALSE
Write the letter for the best answer.   Write T for true and F for false.

1. _____ What is the name of the fifth grade teacher?
   A. Mr. Smith   B. Miss Jones
   C. Mr. Turner   D. Mrs. Myers
2. _____ How many students are in the fifth grade class?
   A. 31   B. 10
   C. 8   D. 20
3. _____ Who won the heat race?
   A. John   B. Leslie
   C. Jess   D. Gary
4. _____ Who was the best runner of the fourth graders?
   A. Ben   B. Billy
   C. Bobby Miller   D. Joseph

1. _____ Leslie has gone to Lark Creek Elementary school since kindergarten.

2. _____ The fifth grade class was very small, it only had 15 students.

3. _____ Jess really liked Leslie and sat next to her on the bus.

4. _____ It is said that Mrs. Myers had never been seen to smile, except the first day of school and the last day of school.

Lesson 2
Write full sentences for this section:

1. Who introduced Leslie to the fifth grade class?
2. What upset the fifth grade teacher?
3. Where did the race take place?
4. When Leslie entered the class, what did she find?
5. Why did the class have lunch at their desks?
6. How was Leslie dressed the first day of school?

(Who) _____

(What) _____

(Where) _____

(When) _____

(Why) _____

(How) _____

LESSON 3
FILL IN THE BLANKS / COMPREHENSION
Write the word to complete the sentence. / Write a full sentence to answer the questions.

Words: melodic rumpus territory contempt worse

1. Each day was _____ than the day before.
2. The spring bubbled up with almost a _____ sound.
3. But Leslie had other problems that caused more of a _____ than lack of money.
4. The sounds of disbelief were already building into a rumbling of _____.
5. They'd kill her for sitting in their _____.

MULTIPLE CHOICE / TRUE AND FALSE
Write the letter for the best answer. / Write T for true and F for false.

1. _____ Who asked to see Jess' drawings?
   A. Mrs. West   B. Mr. Taylor
   C. Miss Edmunds   D. Leslie
2. _____ What did Leslie write her composition about?
   A. singing   B. scuba diving
   C. dancing   D. farming
3. _____ What did Leslie bribe May Belle with?
   A. crayons   B. colored pencils
   C. a ball   D. paper dolls
4. _____ What did Leslie name their secret place?
   A. Terabithia   B. Castlewood
   B. Castle Place   D. New Castle

1. _____ Leslie tripped Janice Avery on the bus, not Jess.

2. _____ Leslie and Jess created a secret place in the Perkins backyard.

3. _____ Leslie did not own a television.

4. _____ Running wasn't fun anymore, and it was all Leslie's fault.

Lesson 3
Write full sentences for this section:

1. Who joined the boys at recess, and won the race everyday?
2. What homework assignment did Mrs. Myers give the class?
3. Where did Leslie and Jess create their secret place?
4. When did school start?
5. Why was recess the only thing Jess looked forward to?
6. How did Leslie's parents earn a living?

(Who) _____

(What) _____

(Where) _____

(When) _____

(Why) _____

(How) _____

LESSON 4
FILL IN THE BLANKS / COMPREHENSION
Write the word to complete the sentence. / Write a full sentence to answer the questions.

Words: tangle   unfortunately   deserves   shuffling   prideful

1. May Belle, _____, was a slow learner.
2. He'd sooner _____ with Mrs. Godzilla herself.
3. She closed the door and left him _____ through each desk.
4. She _____ everything she gets and then some.
5. Jess could see Janice's face all pink and _____.

MULTIPLE CHOICE / TRUE AND FALSE
Write the letter for the best answer. / Write T for true and F for false.

1. _____ Who was the real giant in Jess and Leslie's lives?
   A. Mr. Burke   B. Mrs. Myers
   C. Mr. Taylor   D. Janice Avery
2. _____ What are the names of Janice Avery's friends?
   A. Wilma and Bobby Sue B. Jane and Angela
   C. Ginger and Joan   D. Janet and Edna
3. _____ What grade is May Belle in?
   A. fifth grade   B. kindergarten
   C. first grade   D. third grade
4. _____ What does Janice Avery do in the girls' room?
   A. combed her hair   B. smoked
   C. ate candy   D. put on make-up

1. _____ Jess decided to beat-up Janice and her friends for taking May Belle's Twinkies.

2. _____ Janice knew the note was a trick and threw it away.

3. _____ After school Janice gave May Belle her Twinkies back.

4. _____ May Belle was pleased with Jess and Leslie's revenge on Janice.

Lesson 4
Write full sentences for this section:

1. Who were the school's bullies?
2. What did they do to May Belle?
3. Where did the bullies stand every morning to make the little girls give them their milk money?
4. When did Jess and Leslie put the note in Janice's desk?
5. Why did Leslie go ahead of Jess in the hallway?
6. How did Jess like Leslie's stories?

(Who) _____
_____
_____
_____

(What) _____
_____
_____
_____

(Where) _____
_____
_____
_____

(When) _____
_____
_____
_____

(Why) _____
_____
_____
_____

(How) _____
_____
_____
_____

LESSON 5
FILL IN THE BLANKS / COMPREHENSION
Write the word to complete the sentence. / Write a full sentence to answer the questions.

Words: sense   foundling   obsessed   imitated   guardian

1. Christmas was a month away, but at Jesse's house the girls were already _____ with it.
2. Nobody with any _____ could call that stick a girl.
3. Maybe I was a _____, like in the stories.
4. Everything the dog did, he _____.
5. How will we teach him to be a noble _____?

MULTIPLE CHOICE / TRUE AND FALSE
Write the letter for the best answer. / Write T for true and F for false.

1. _____ What did Jess give Leslie for Christmas?
   A. a puppy   B. a lizard
   C. a cat   D. a fish bowl
2. _____ What did Leslie name the puppy?
   A. Spot   B. Chip
   C. Prince Terrien   D. Buddy
3. _____ What did May Belle get for a present?
   A. a ball   B. a stuffed bear
   C. books   D. a Barbie doll
4. _____ What did Dad give Jess for Christmas?
   A. new boots   B. electric racing-car set
   C. toy boat   D. crayons

1. _____ Mr. and Mrs. Burke were not happy about having a puppy to worry about.

2. _____ Jess was excited about the gift Leslie gave him.

3. _____ Jesse's Dad was disappointed with the racing-car set.

4. _____ That night the glow of that afternoon stayed with Jess.

Lesson 5
Write full sentences for this section:

1. Who was waiting for Jess on Christmas morning at Bessie's shed?
2. What did Leslie give Jess for Christmas?
3. Where did Jess meet Leslie on Christmas Eve?
4. When they met at the castle stronghold, what did they do?
5. Why did Joyce Ann cry about Santa coming?
6. How could Jess and the puppy have bad luck?

(Who) _____
_____
_____
_____

(What) _____
_____
_____
_____

(Where) _____
_____
_____
_____

(When) _____
_____
_____
_____

(Why) _____
_____
_____
_____

(How) _____
_____
_____
_____

LESSON 6
FILL IN THE BLANKS / COMPREHENSION
Write the word to complete the sentence. / Write a full sentence to answer the questions.

Words: nuisance   tantrum   absentminded   trick   reluctant

1. Mr. Burke was inclined to be _____.
2. Jess found he was useful to him, not a _____ to be tolerated.
3. They'll _____ new clothes out of somebody.
4. It was like Brenda throwing a _____ over Joyce Ann touching her lipstick.
5. It was plain the magic was _____ to come to him.

MULTIPLE CHOICE / TRUE AND FALSE
Write the letter for the best answer. / Write T for true and F for false.

1. _____ After Christmas, what was Mr. Burke busy with?
   A. repairing his house   B. writing a new book
   C. listening to music   D. painting a portrait
2. _____ Who made Terabithia magic for Jess?
   A. Mom   B. Dad
   C. May Belle   D. Leslie
3. _____ Mr. Burke wanted Jess to call him _____.
   A. William   B. neighbor
   C. Bill   D. Mr. Burke
4. _____ Who was laid-off before Easter?
   A. the postman   B. Jesse's Dad
   C. Mrs. Myers   D. Mr. Turner

1. _____ Jesse's Mom would not allow Leslie to go to church with them.

2. _____ Jesse's family went to church every Sunday morning.

3. _____ "All the Burkes were smart," Jess thought.

4. _____ Prince Terrien's nickname is P.T.

Lesson 6
Write full sentences for this section:

1. Who was crying in the girl's room at school?
2. What did Leslie wear to church on Easter?
3. Where did May Belle follow Jess and Leslie to?
4. When church was over, how did Leslie feel?
5. Why was Leslie so happy to help her Dad with the house repairs?
6. How did Mr. Burke feel about Jess?

(Who) _____
_____
_____

(What) _____
_____
_____

(Where) _____
_____
_____

(When) _____
_____
_____

(Why) _____
_____
_____

(How) _____
_____
_____

LESSON 7
FILL IN THE BLANKS / COMPREHENSION
Write the word to complete the sentence. / Write a full sentence to answer the questions.

Words: arise   hesitate   conspiring   perceive   sporadically

1. It was as though the elements were _____ to ruin their short week.
2. _____ King of Terabithia, and let us proceed into our kingdom.
3. The rain continued _____ so that the creek had swollen to the trunk of the apple tree.
4. Leslie never seemed to _____, so Jess could not hang back.
5. For a truth, I _____ this is no ordinary rain falling on our kingdom.

MULTIPLE CHOICE / TRUE AND FALSE
Write the letter for the best answer. / Write T for true and F for false.

1. _____ On Easter, how was the weather?
   A. hot   B. heavy rain
   C. frosty   D. sunny
2. _____ What did Lesley want to do that day?
   A. go to school   B. go to the mall
   C. go to Terabithia   D. go to church
3. _____ What is Leslie's mother's name?
   A. Judy   B. Sandy
   C. Alice   D. Karen
4. _____ What did Leslie's mother write?
   A. children's poetry   B. newspapers
   C. magazines   D. novels

1. _____ With the rain, the creek began to overflow.

2. _____ Jess and Leslie changed their minds and went to Jesse's house to watch T.V.

3. _____ Jess and Leslie left P.T. at Leslie's house, instead of taking him with them.

4. _____ Because of the rain, Jess and Leslie never were able to visit Terabithia

Lesson 7
Write full sentences for this section:

1. Who used to like to walk in the rain?
2. What made Jess think about the movie, "The Ten Commandments"?
3. Where did Jess and Leslie want to go in the rain?
4. When Jess was in the pine grove, what did he think of?
5. Why did Leslie say she wanted to go to the pine forest?
6. How did Leslie and Jess cross the overflowing creek?

(Who) _____
_____
_____
_____

(What) _____
_____
_____
_____

(Where) _____
_____
_____
_____

(When) _____
_____
_____
_____

(Why) _____
_____
_____
_____

(How) _____
_____
_____
_____

LESSON 8
FILL IN THE BLANKS / COMPREHENSION
Write the word to complete the sentence. / Write a full sentence to answer the questions.

Words: permission scrawny liberated absorbed guts

1. May Belle was as _____ as Brenda was fat.
2. He may not have been born with _____, but he didn't have to die without them.
3. Do you need to get _____?
4. He was glad May Belle was _____ in the T.V.
5. The war _____ the country from tyranny.

MULTIPLE CHOICE / TRUE AND FALSE
Write the letter for the best answer. / Write T for true and F for false.

1. _____ Who called to invite Jess on a trip to Washington?
   A. Miss Edmunds   B. Leslie
   C. Mr. Turner   D. Dad
2. _____ Where did Miss Edmunds take Jess?
   A. Lincoln Memorial   B. White house
   C. Smithsonian   D. National Gallery
3. _____ Where did they go after lunch?
   A. an old bridge   B. an old mansion
   C. Smithsonian   D. Library of Congress
4. _____ What did they see at the Smithsonian?
   A. plants and trees   B. dinosaurs and Indian relics
   C. boats and ships   D. African Violets

1. _____ Leslie had a wonderful time with Miss Edmunds and Jess in Washington.

2. _____ Miss Edmunds had gone to college in Japan for one year.

3. _____ When Jess came home, he realized something was terribly wrong at home.

4. _____ Jess had been to Washington many times with his Dad.

Lesson 8
Write full sentences for this section:

1. Who was found dead, while Jess was gone to Washington?
2. What did Jesse's family think happened to Jess?
3. Where was Jesse's Dad that morning?
4. When Jess asked his mother to go with Miss Edmunds, was she totally awake?
5. Why did his family think he was dead?
6. How did Jess know something was wrong at his house?

(Who) _____
_____
_____
_____

(What) _____
_____
_____
_____

(Where) _____
_____
_____
_____

(When) _____
_____
_____
_____

(Why) _____
_____
_____
_____

(How) _____
_____
_____
_____

LESSON 9
FILL IN THE BLANKS / COMPREHENSION
Write the word to complete the sentence. / Write a full sentence to answer the questions.

Words: numbness   doused   threatened   accusation   dreadful

1. He got out, and with the cold _____ spreading through him, went to lie on his bed.
2. He remembered that as being part of the _____ dream.
3. The sky _____ to pour down rain.
4. It wasn't an _____.
5. He _____ them with syrup and began to eat.

MULTIPLE CHOICE / TRUE AND FALSE
Write the letter for the best answer. / Write T for true and F for false.

1. _____ Who took over Jessie's chores?
   A. Brenda   B. May Belle
   C. Mom   D. Dad
2. _____ Where did they find Leslie's body?
   A. in the backyard   B. in the creek
   C. in the street   D. in the woods
3. _____ Who tried to comfort Jess, as he ran down the street?
   A. his Dad   B. May Belle
   C. Mom   D. Mr. Burke
4. _____ Mom made what for Jessie's breakfast?
   A. oatmeal   B. eggs
   C. pancakes   D. cold cereal

1. _____ Jess could not understand that Leslie was dead.

2. _____ P.T., Leslie's dog, had been with Leslie at the creek.

3. _____ Leslie and Jess had never been at Terabithia in the dark.

4. _____ Jess could not understand how Leslie could drown because she was a good swimmer.

Lesson 9
Write full sentences for this section:

1. Who told Jess about Leslie's accident?
2. What did Jess think when he awoke from sleep?
3. Where did Jess run to when he ran out the door?
4. When Jessie's Dad told him about Leslie, what did Jess say to his Dad?
5. Why did Jess feel it was his fault that Leslie was dead?
6. How did Leslie die?

(Who) _____

(What) _____

(Where) _____

(When) _____

(Why) _____

(How) _____

LESSON 10.
FILL IN THE BLANKS / COMPREHENSION
Write the word to complete the sentence. / Write a full sentence to answer the questions.

Words: examined weird constricting wreath evidence

1. There was something _____ about the sound coming from the shed.
2. The man picked up the box and _____ it carefully.
3. There was no _____ to suggest that the queen had died.
4. The fear had moved up into his throat, _____ it.
5. We must make a funeral _____ for the queen.

MULTIPLE CHOICE / TRUE AND FALSE
Write the letter for the best answer. / Write T for true and F for false.

1. _____ Who did Bill ask to care for P.T.?
   A. Jessie   B. Mr. Turner
   C. Miss Edmunds   D. Mrs. Myers
2. _____ Where were the Burkes taking Leslie's ashes?
   A. New Jersey   B. Washington
   C. Pennsylvania   D. New York
3. _____ In Jessie's sadness, who did he hit?
   A. Brenda   B. Mom
   C. Dad   D. May Belle
4. _____ What did Jessie go looking for Saturday morning?
   A. Miss Bessie, the cow B. the paints Leslie gave him
   C. wildflowers   D. a book

1. _____ Jess made a bridge out of old wood from Leslie's house.

2. _____ Jess found his paints at the creek.

3. _____ Jessie felt that Leslie belonged to him.

4. _____ Leslie's Grandmother knew about Jess, because Leslie told her about him.

Lesson 10
Write full sentences for this section:

1. Who followed Jess to the creek to comfort him?
2. What happened to Bill and Judy?
3. Where did Jess find May Belle when he returned from the sacred grove?
4. When he returned to school, who needed comfort along with Jess?
5. Why had the Burkes moved to the old Perkins' place in the first place?
6. How did Jess make a funeral wreath for Leslie?

(Who) _____

(What) _____

(Where) _____

(When) _____

(Why) _____

(How) _____

ANSWER KEY:

Lesson 1

Vocabulary

Fill in the blanks.

1. figured
2. taste
3. cuds
4. grits
5. peculiar

Comprehension Who, What, Where, When, Why, and How

1. A family named Burke
2. Running
3. Around the cow field
4. Crazy animals with problems
5. He wanted to be the fastest runner in the 5th grade at school.
6. He put his beasts into impossible fixes.

Comprehension Multiple Choice

1. A
2. C
3. D
4. B

Comprehension True and False

1. T
2. F
3. T
4. F

Lesson 2

Vocabulary

Fill in the blanks.

1. reaction
2. retreating
3. snottiest
4. repulsive
5. sarcasm

Comprehension Who, What, Where, When, Why, and How

1. Mr. Taylor
2. Her class was the largest in the school.
3. The schools upper field
4. A small basement with five rows of six desks already filled
5. The school didn't have a lunchroom.
6. She wore faded cutoffs, a blue undershirt, and sneakers with no socks.

Comprehension Multiple Choice

1. D
2. A
3. B
4. C

Comprehension True and False

1. F
2. F
3. F
4. T

Lesson 3.
Vocabulary
Fill in the blanks.
1. worse
2. melodic
3. rumpus
4. contempt
5. territory
Comprehension Who, What, Where, When, Why, and How
1. Leslie Burke
2. They were to watch a T.V. program about Jasques Cousteau.
3. In the woods where no one could mess it up
4. The first Tuesday after Labor Day
5. Leslie was always funny and made the long days bearable.
6. Both were book writers.
Comprehension Multiple Choice
1. C
2. B
3. D
4. A
Comprehension True and False
1. F
2. F
3. T
4. T

Lesson 4.
Vocabulary
Fill in the blanks.
1. unfortunately
2. tangle
3. shuffling
4. deserves
5. prideful
Comprehension Who, What, Where, When, Why, and How
1. Janice Avery, Wilma Dean, and Bobby Sue Henshaw
2. They stole her Twinkies.
3. Outside the girls' bathroom.
4. Before the first morning bell
5. Mr. Turner was death on students sneaking around the halls.
6. He loved them.
Comprehension Multiple Choice
1. D
2. A
3. C
4. B
Comprehension True and False
1. F
2. F
3. F
4. T

Lesson 5
Vocabulary
Fill in the blanks.
1. obsessed
2. sense
3. foundling
4. imitated
5. guardian
Comprehension Who, What, Where, When, Why, and How
1. Leslie and Prince Terrien
2. A box of watercolors, brushes, and heavy art paper
3. At the castle stronghold
4. Exchange Christmas gifts
5. They had no fireplace and Santa wouldn't find the house.
6. Jess must enter Terabithia only by swinging across the creek; any other way would bring bad luck.
Comprehension Multiple Choice
1. A
2. C
3. D
4. B
Comprehension True and False
1. F
2. T
3. T
4. T

Lesson 6
Vocabulary
Fill in the blanks.
1. absentminded
2. nuisance
3. trick
4. tantrum
5. reluctant
Comprehension Who, What, Where, When, Why, and How
1. Janice Avery
2. A navy-blue jumper over a blouse with tiny flowers and shiny brown leather shoes
3. To their hiding place in the woods
4. She was glad she came, and found it interesting.
5. She was learning to understand her father.
6. He thought Jess was amazing.
Comprehension Multiple Choice
1. A
2. D
3. C
4. B
Comprehension True and False
1. F
2. F
3. T
4. T

Lesson 7
Vocabulary
Fill in the blanks.
1. conspiring
2. arise
3. sporadically
4. hesitate
5. perceive

Comprehension Who, What, Where, When, Why, and How
1. Leslie's mother
2. The dry bed of the creek was like a roaring eight-foot-wide sea.
3. To Terabithia
4. Dry clothes and a cup of hot coffee in front of the T.V
5. She thought some evil put a curse on her kingdom.
6. They used the old rope on the crabapple tree.

Comprehension Multiple Choice
1. B
2. C
3. A
4. D

Comprehension True and False
1. T
2. F
3. F
4. F

Lesson 8
Vocabulary
Fill in the blanks.
1. scrawny
2. guts
3. permission
4. absorbed
5. liberated

Comprehension Who, What, Where, When, Why, and How
1. Leslie
2. They thought he was dead.
3. He was gone early that morning looking for work.
4. No, she was half asleep.
5. Leslie was found dead, and they thought Jess was with her.
6. The family was sitting at the kitchen table, not eating or looking at T.V., and his mom was crying.

Comprehension Multiple Choice
1. A
2. D
3. C
4. B

Comprehension True and False
1. F
2. T
3. T
4. F

Lesson 9
Vocabulary
Fill in the blanks.
1. numbness
2. dreadful
3. threatened
4. accusation
5. doused

Comprehension Who, What, Where, When, Why, and How
1. Dad
2. He thought everything that happened that day was just a dreadful dream.
3. He ran down the road west away from the old Perkins' place.
4. No, you're lying to me.
5. He had not invited her to go to Washington with him and Miss Edmunds.
6. The old rope broke and Leslie hit her head on something when she fell.

Comprehension Multiple Choice
1. D
2. B
3. A
4. C

Comprehension True and False
1. T
2. F
3. T
4. T

Lesson 10
Vocabulary
Fill in the blanks.
1. weird
2. examined
3. evidence
4. constricting
5. wreath

Comprehension Who, What, Where, When, Why, and How
1. Dad
2. They moved back to Pennsylvania.
3. She was halfway across the tree bridge, afraid to move.
4. Mrs. Myers
5. They moved to the country for Leslie's sake.
6. He bent a pine bough into a circle, tied it, and wove wildflowers into it.

Comprehension Multiple Choice
1. A
2. C
3. D
4. B

Comprehension True and False
1. T
2. F
3. T
4. T